Cooking Texas Style

Cooking Texas Style

A Heritage of Traditional Recipes

by Candy Wagner and Sandra Marquez

UNIVERSITY OF TEXAS PRESS ❦ AUSTIN

Second Printing, 1983

Requests for permission to reproduce material
from this work should be sent to:
  Permissions
  University of Texas Press
  Box 7819
  Austin, Texas 78712

Library of Congress Cataloging in Publication Data

Wagner, Candy, 1946–
  Cooking Texas style: a heritage of traditional recipes.
  Includes index.
  1. Cookery, American—Texas. 2. Texas—Social life and
customs. I. Marquez, Sandra, 1948– . II. Title.
TX715.W137 1983   641.5   82-7060
ISBN 0-292-71082-8   AACR2

Illustrations by Melissa Grimes

To our grandmother, Hertha Bremer Erben,
one of our greatest inspirations in life
and certainly in cooking— we thought of her
and missed her even more while writing this book.

To our grandmother, Mary McClaugherty Orndorff Schmidt,
who spreads love and life to all of those around her—
we are thankful for her each day.

Contents

Acknowledgments

A very special thanks to our parents, Dona and Harvey Erben, for the idea, support, help, love, and our childhood of Texas cooking and to our aunt, Almira Conway, for her tireless help. For their contributions we also thank our brother, Randy Erben, family members Nell Livingston, Pauline Lusson, Gertrude Walker, Nora and Doyle Wagner, and Barry Bibb and our friend Camille Becker.

Introduction

It has been said that there are two kinds of people in the world:
Texans and those who want to be. It has been said, as well, that
Texans have a tendency to tell "tall tales" and exaggerate a bit,
and the first statement probably fits into this category. However,
Texans enjoy a lifestyle that has great appeal: a casual elegance
with good times, good food, and carefree entertaining. We would
like to share this feeling of Texas and hope that through these
pages you will find not only a collection of recipes but a way of life
that can be adapted anywhere.

Part of the appeal and uniqueness of Texas comes from its variety. Within its boundaries there are dust-blown plains in the Pan-
handle, golden sun-drenched beaches on the Gulf Coast, verdant
pine forests to the east, and desert sands and rugged mountains to
the west. The cultures and traditions are as varied as the topogra-
phy, and these variations are exemplified in "Texas food."

Some background may be helpful in explaining the influences of
these various cultures as well as why these recipes, passed to us
through the generations, are considered staples of the Lone Star
State.

This background begins with John Coker, a young man who left
his native state of Alabama in the early 1830's for the wide open
spaces of what is now known as Texas. John found himself in the
middle of the Texas Revolution and joined Sam Houston's forces at
the Battle of San Jacinto. Under General Houston's orders, John
Coker and six other men led by Erastus "Deaf" Smith were sent
out to destroy Vince's Bridge. They accomplished their mission on
the morning of April 21, 1836. With this bridge destroyed, General
Santa Anna and his Mexican army were trapped. Later that after-

noon, General Houston and his army made a surprise attack and, with no place to retreat, Santa Anna and his men were defeated. It was this battle that won Texas its independence from Mexico.

Those who fought were rewarded with gifts of land. The Texas Legislature gave John Coker one-third league of land (1,920 acres) situated in what is now San Antonio. John, a bachelor, sent for his family in Alabama. One of his brothers, Joseph Coker, with his wife and their eight children, began the trek by covered wagon to join him. Joseph's wife died during the trip, and he and the children continued the journey, arriving in Texas in 1840. They settled on part of the land which had been given to John. Here our great-great-great-great-uncle John and great-great-great-grandfather Joseph began a new life. Even today, that area in north San Antonio is known as the Coker Settlement.

Our next ancestor to arrive in Texas was Heinrich Conrad Friedrich Christian Bremer, who sailed from Verden, Germany, with his wife, Judith Annette Christiane Bremer, and five children and landed at Galveston on November 22, 1844. One more child was born during the voyage. Heinrich was a member of the Society for the Protection of German Immigrants in Texas, and this entitled him to a piece of good land—the size according to the number in his family. After arriving in Galveston, the family sailed to Port Lavaca on Matagorda Bay. From there they made their way north by wagon until, on March 21, 1845, they reached their settlement—New Braunfels, Texas. Heinrich Bremer is listed as one of the founding fathers of New Braunfels, and there and in the surrounding areas he helped to settle over 135 years ago his descendants have lived ever since. Today, living in San Antonio, we are only twenty-five miles south of the place our great-great-great-grandfather Heinrich helped to settle over 135 years ago.

Other members of our family came to Texas more recently. Our paternal grandfather, Adolph Erben, was a descendant of a former Catholic priest who came from Austria to Texas. Adolph married Hertha Bremer, Heinrich Bremer's great-granddaughter. Our maternal grandfather, Hurcell Paul Orndorff, came to Texas in 1916 after joining the army in New York. His express purpose in coming to Texas was to help capture Pancho Villa. He met and married Mary Adeline McClaugherty, Joseph Coker's great-granddaughter. Mary's father, John McClaugherty, was a descendant of James McClaugherty, who came to America from Ireland in 1786.

The story of our family is not unique; it is characteristic of many pioneer Texas families. Texas became a great cultural "melting pot." First there were the Indians; then the early Spanish, French, and Mexican colonizers; then immigrants from all over the United States and Europe. From this mixture of cultures and peoples came Texas food and eating customs which we know and cherish today. The predominant influences today are those of the German, Deep South, and Spanish/Mexican cultures.

We learned from our German heritage that mealtime is an important part of the day, not only for sustenance but as a time for family and friends to keep in touch. We are ever mindful of the fact that love and care should go into the preparation of food, whether the preparation takes five minutes or five hours. Then, when it is prepared, everyone, including the cook, should sit down and leisurely enjoy the meal as a celebration of life and in gratitude for the bounty on the table.

The Deep South influence gave us much more than cornbread and grits. The hospitality the South is so famous for and its easygoing ways are an integral part of Texas.

The southern lifestyle complements the Spanish/Mexican influence in Texas, where the slogan "mi casa es su casa" (my house is your house) is said with sincerity. The foods and cooking techniques adapted from our Mexican neighbors are, to most Texans, indispensable, as is the relaxed attitude about life which we share.

The appreciation and awareness of our past contributes much to our modern life. However, there are also many advantages to cooking in the 1980's. What took Grandma hours to do can now be done in minutes without sacrificing authenticity, good taste, or hours of the day. A Texas cook can be as relaxed with a party for forty as with four and should have just as good a time as any of the guests. A spur-of-the-moment party is a delight and, with the host at ease, the get-together goes as if planned for weeks.

This blending of old and new is the most important factor which contributes to the "casual elegance" and down-home goodness of Texas food and entertaining. It is this feeling we want to share.

To the Reader

This book is a compilation of Texas recipes handed down through generations; it is not intended to provide all the foods needed for a daily diet. We hope that our readers will follow a healthful and sensible diet that can include many of our recipes but will also contain fresh fruits, vegetables, and whole grains. We also hope that readers using these recipes will feel free to change the type of oil or decrease the amount of sugar or salt called for to comply with their individual dietary needs. We have in general tried to avoid the use of highly processed foods or foods with additives such as artificial coloring, artificial flavor, or preservatives.

Notes on Ingredients

On green chilies: The canned green chilies called for in several recipes are Poblano peppers which have been roasted and peeled as in the recipe for Rajas (in Chapter 6). The roasting and peeling is a time-consuming, tedious task, and the fresh Poblano peppers are frequently unavailable; so we have generally specified the canned chilies, which are readily available and of good quality, without additives. However, the fresh, roasted and peeled chilies may be substituted in all cases.

On jalapeños: Fresh jalapeño peppers are specified in some recipes and canned jalapeños in others. Except where it is indicated that either kind may be used, these should not be substituted for one another. The canned peppers are pickled and are quite different from the fresh.

Cooking Texas Style

1. Appetizers

Beer Cheese Spread

The beer gives this spread a delicious flavor, and it is a great recipe to make ahead and keep on hand for impromptu entertaining. Store it in small crocks or jars and refrigerate. It will keep for up to 6 weeks. Just bring the cheese to room temperature before serving. The spread makes a wonderful gift, and with the use of a food processor it can be whipped up in almost no time.

1 pound Cheddar cheese	1 clove garlic, pressed
1 pound Swiss cheese	1 teaspoon Worcestershire sauce
1 teaspoon dry mustard	1 12-ounce can beer

Finely grate cheeses and place in a large mixing bowl. Add mustard, garlic, and Worcestershire sauce and toss well to distribute seasonings. Add beer, mixing well, until the cheese is of a spreadable consistency. YIELD: *5 cups*

Borracho Bean Dip

When pinto beans and beer are combined, the beans literally drink up the beer, making them *frijoles borrachos*, or "drunk beans." Borracho (bo-RA-cho) Bean Dip is a good way to use the last of any leftover beans; it can also be made with canned refried beans.

2 tablespoons bacon drippings (oil may be substituted)
1 small onion, chopped
2 cups cooked pinto beans
½ pound Cheddar cheese, grated
½ cup canned jalapeños, seeded and chopped
½ cup beer
salt to taste
shredded cheese for garnish

Sauté onion in bacon drippings or oil in a large skillet over medium high heat. Add the cooked beans, mashing them as they heat, until they are not quite smooth. Reduce heat to low and add grated cheese, jalapeños, beer, and salt. Cook until all ingredients are heated through and cheese melts.

Garnish with shredded cheese and serve warm with tostados or corn chips.   YIELD: *4 cups*

Con Queso

The Spanish words *con queso* (kohn KEH-soh) mean "with cheese," and Texans use Con Queso with a myriad of different foods. It is primarily a cheese dip which is served warm with corn chips or tostados. It can also be used as a sauce over grilled steaks, as a substitute for cheese sauce over vegetables, dribbled over a chalupa, or spread on a meat pattie to make Burgers con Queso, just to give a few examples.

3 tablespoons vegetable oil
3 tablespoons flour
1½ cups evaporated milk
2 pounds Monterrey Jack, Longhorn, or Cheddar cheese, grated
1 cup canned tomatoes, with juice
1 cup canned green chilies, chopped
salt to taste (optional)

In a double boiler, combine oil and flour. Slowly add evaporated milk to make a thick cream sauce. Add the grated cheese and cook over low heat until the cheese is melted. Add tomatoes and chilies, breaking up the tomatoes as you add them. Stir until well blended and creamy. Season with salt, if desired. Serve warm with tostados.   YIELD: *4 cups*

Paresa

When the Mexican influence and steak tartare were combined, Texas came up with Paresa. Serve it with crackers or toast rounds and plenty of cold beer. Any leftover Paresa can be made into meatballs or patties and cooked as desired. The patties make great burgers.

5 pounds ground sirloin, very lean	**salt and pepper to taste**
2½ pounds Longhorn or Cheddar	**cayenne pepper to taste**
cheese, grated	**juice of 6 lemons**
1 large onion, finely chopped	**parsley for garnish**
2 cloves garlic, minced	**sliced onion rings for garnish**

In a large bowl, combine ground sirloin, grated cheese, chopped onion, garlic, salt, pepper, and cayenne, mixing well. Add lemon juice and blend thoroughly.

Refrigerate for several hours before serving. When ready to serve, mound the Paresa on a tray and garnish with parsley and sliced onion rings.   YIELD: *16–20 servings*

Picadillo

Texans are known for their easy, carefree style of entertaining. The main ingredient that makes this work is the flexibility of the host or hostess. Often friends drop by at the spur of the moment for a short visit which turns into a fun-filled evening. With the right foods on hand, this does not have to mean hours in the kitchen or a full course meal. Picadillo (pee-kah-DEE-yoh) is a hearty, robust meat dip with a wonderful blend of flavors, which can be made ahead and refrigerated for a week or frozen for up to three months, ready and waiting for just such an occasion. Simply heat and serve with tostados or corn chips or spoon into warmed flour tortillas. It is guaranteed to take the edge off the biggest appetite.

1 pound ground beef
1 pound ground pork
4 large tomatoes
4 green onions, finely chopped
1 cup diced pimiento
1 cup slivered almonds
2 cloves garlic, minced

12 ounces tomato paste
4 canned jalapeños, seeded and
    chopped
1 cup raisins
1 teaspoon ground cumin
    (comino)
1 teaspoon oregano

Brown beef and pork in a large pan over high heat, separating
with a fork, until cooked through. Lower heat to medium and place
whole tomatoes on top of meat. Cover and let simmer 10–15 minutes. Remove tomatoes, peel and dice them, and return to pan
with their juice. Stir in remaining ingredients and mix well. Cover
and simmer for 20–30 minutes or until the mixture is well blended
and the raisins are plump.   YIELD: *12–18 servings*

Chili Nuts

Sometimes called Picosos, meaning "hot ones," Chili Nuts are a
great snack and the perfect accompaniment for an ice-cold beer.
Adjust the degree of "hot" by adding more or less cayenne pepper.
If stored in an air-tight container, these will keep fresh for several
weeks.

4 tablespoons peanut oil or butter
1 pound raw peanuts, shelled
4 teaspoons chili powder

¾ teaspoon paprika
2 teaspoons salt
½–1 teaspoon cayenne pepper

Place oil or butter in a large, shallow baking pan. Add the peanuts
and toss to coat evenly. Spread nuts in a single layer and bake at
300° for 30 minutes, stirring occasionally.

Combine remaining ingredients. After the nuts have baked for
30 minutes, remove them from the oven, sprinkle them with seasoning mixture, and toss well. Return them to the oven and continue baking for 30 more minutes. Allow to cool and drain on paper
towels.   YIELD: *1 pound*

Salted Pecans

In the fall, when the pecan tree branches begin to droop under the weight of a bumper crop of nuts, you can look forward to Salted Pecans as snacks or packaged for holiday gift-giving, as they will keep for several weeks in an air-tight container.

4 tablespoons butter
1 pound shelled pecans

1 tablespoon salt
¼ teaspoon white pepper

Melt the butter in a large, shallow baking pan. Add pecans and stir to coat evenly. Spread pecans in a single layer and bake at 300° for 30 minutes, stirring occasionally, being careful not to overcook.

Sprinkle with salt and pepper and toss well. Cool the pecans in the pan. When cool, drain on paper towels. YIELD: *5 cups*

Stuffed Jalapeños

There are some people, even in Texas, who cannot tolerate the fiery hot, green jewel, the jalapeño (hal-a-PAIN-yo) pepper, at its full strength but who do enjoy its unique flavor. Stuffed Jalapeños is an example of a way to have the best of both worlds. If the veins and seeds are removed and the peppers rinsed well, much of the fire disappears, leaving a tasty treat. Serve them as an appetizer, as a garnish, or as a special addition to a relish tray.

12 canned jalapeño peppers
4 ounces cream cheese
1 tablespoon sour cream

¼ teaspoon garlic salt
1 tablespoon finely chopped onion
paprika

Cut each pepper in half lengthwise, remove veins and seeds, and drain. Mash the softened cream cheese with the sour cream; stir in garlic salt and onion. Stuff each pepper half with the cheese mixture and sprinkle lightly with paprika. Chill before serving.

YIELD: *2 dozen*

Fried Jalapeños

In Texas it is said that the jalapeño can cure a myriad of illnesses from sinus headaches to ulcers. If so, then Texans should be the healthiest people around, for jalapeños are consumed in abundance in every way, shape, and form. One of these forms is Fried Jalapeños, which are an example of something so good that it does not matter how hot it is.

20–24 canned jalapeño peppers	**1 tablespoon vegetable oil**
½ cup yellow cornmeal	**1 cup beer**
1 cup flour	**oil for frying**
1 teaspoon baking powder	**3–4 ounces Muenster cheese**
½ teaspoon salt	**½ cup flour**

Make a small slit in each pepper. Remove the seeds and membranes, being careful to keep the pepper from tearing. Rinse each pepper with cold water and drain well.

In a small mixing bowl combine the cornmeal, 1 cup flour, baking powder, and salt. Add 1 tablespoon oil and the beer and mix until smooth. Allow this batter to rest for 10–15 minutes.

In a small saucepan heat 3 inches of oil to 350°. Cut the cheese in small pieces and use to fill the cavity of each pepper. Roll each pepper in ½ cup flour, dip in batter to cover, and fry in hot oil 1–2 minutes or until golden brown. Drain on paper towels and serve immediately.   YIELD: *20–24*

Fried Potato Skins

Our German heritage taught us about the versatility of the potato, and Fried Potato Skins is certainly an example. They make a delicious side dish as well as tempting appetizers. For an added twist, sprinkle crisp-fried bacon pieces or chopped green chilies over the cheese just before broiling. (Our grandmothers would remind us that the scooped-out potato should be saved for use in Potato Soup—see Chapter 3.) Serve alone or with a dish of sour cream for dipping.

6 medium baking potatoes   salt to taste
oil for frying   1½ cups grated cheese

Wash and scrub potatoes. Dry and wrap each in aluminum foil and bake at 350° for 45–60 minutes or until tender.

When done, cut the potatoes in half, lengthwise. Scoop out the potato, leaving a ¼-inch border of potato around the skin.

Heat 3 inches of oil in a large saucepan to 385°. Fry each potato skin until crisp and golden brown. Drain on paper towels and lightly salt.

Fill each skin with ¼ cup grated cheese. Place skins under the broiler until cheese melts.   YIELD: *6 servings*

Steak Bits

Texans like their beef. Since the early days of the cattle drives, beef has been a mainstay, served for breakfast, lunch, and dinner. A hearty "starter," Steak Bits combines two Texas favorites, beef and beer.

1 cup beer   ½ cup butter
¼ cup olive oil   1 teaspoon dry mustard
2 cloves garlic, pressed   1 teaspoon Worcestershire sauce
2 pounds sirloin steak or round   2 tablespoons red wine
   steak, 2 inches thick   fresh ground pepper to taste

Combine beer, olive oil, and 1 clove of pressed garlic. Pour over steak and marinate for several hours. Reserve the marinade.

Broil or grill the steak to rare or medium rare. Cut in small, bite-size pieces and set aside.

In a saucepan combine the butter, dry mustard, remaining garlic clove, Worcestershire sauce, wine, pepper, and the remaining marinade. Heat slowly until the butter is melted and the sauce is heated through.

To serve, dunk the meat pieces with toothpicks or cocktail forks in the warm sauce, or combine the meat and sauce in a chafing dish and keep warm.   YIELD: *10–12 servings*

Pickled Tongue in Mayonnaise

When we were children, Sunday dinner at Grandmother's house was a very special treat. While she assembled the abundance of food on the table, we would whet our appetites with thinly sliced boiled tongue in a mayonnaise sauce. It was accompanied by a loaf of warm, fresh bread and a big bowl of home-canned dill pickles.

1 pound Boiled Tongue, thinly sliced (see recipe in Chapter 4)
1 large onion, thinly sliced
½ cup vinegar
½ teaspoon salt

1–2 teaspoons coarse ground pepper
1 teaspoon sugar
1 cup mayonnaise

In a nonmetallic bowl, layer sliced tongue and onion. Combine vinegar, salt, pepper, and sugar and pour over the tongue and onion. Cover and refrigerate for several hours or overnight. When ready to serve, pour off the vinegar marinade and add the mayonnaise. Toss lightly, just enough to evenly coat the tongue and onions.   YIELD: *about 2 cups*

Flautas

The Spanish word *flauta* (FLOU-ta), meaning "flute," describes the shape of this crisp, rolled chicken taco. A great finger food, Flautas should be served warm as is or with sour cream, guacamole, or hot sauce.

1 tablespoon oil
2 tablespoons flour
½ cup chicken stock
1 tablespoon finely chopped onion
2 tablespoons chopped canned green chilies

1 cup cooked chicken, finely chopped
½ teaspoon salt
oil for frying
12 corn tortillas

In a small skillet, combine 1 tablespoon oil and flour. Slowly add the chicken stock and cook over medium heat, stirring constantly, to make a smooth cream sauce. Add onions, chilies, chicken, and salt; heat thoroughly and set aside.

Heat ½ inch oil in a skillet over high heat. When the oil is hot, dip each tortilla in oil, using tongs, just long enough to soften (1–2 seconds). Drain on paper towels.

Place 1 heaping tablespoon of the chicken mixture on each tortilla and roll each into a cigar shape. Place on an ungreased, shallow baking pan, seam side down. Bake at 400° for 20 minutes or until crisp.   YIELD: *1 dozen*

Flaquitos

A close kin to Flautas, Flaquitos (flah-KEE-toes) have a savory beef filling. They can easily be used for a main course dish, allowing two or three per serving.

1 small onion, grated	1 tablespoon hot sauce
½ pound ground beef	oil for frying
1 teaspoon salt	18 corn tortillas
1 teaspoon ground cumin	2 cups Longhorn or Cheddar
(comino)	cheese, grated
1 clove garlic, crushed	

In a heavy skillet, sauté onion and beef until the beef is browned and the onion wilted. Add salt, cumin, garlic, and hot sauce. Simmer over medium heat for 3–5 minutes.

Heat ½ inch oil in a small skillet over high heat. When oil is hot, dip each tortilla in oil, using tongs, just enough to soften them (1–2 seconds).

Place approximately 1 tablespoon meat mixture and 2 tablespoons grated cheese on each tortilla. Roll each in a cigar shape and place on an ungreased, shallow baking pan, seam side down. Bake at 400° for 20 minutes or until crisp.   YIELD: *18*

Nachos

The state bird of Texas is the mockingbird, the state flower is the bluebonnet, and the state appetizer, if there were such a thing, would be Nachos. They are served in many different ways all across the state, but the basic Nacho is a corn tortilla chip topped with cheese and a jalapeño slice.

6 corn tortillas
oil for frying

¼ pound Monterrey Jack, Long-
horn, or Cheddar cheese
1 or 2 canned jalapeño peppers

Cut tortillas in quarters. Heat 1 inch of oil in a small skillet over high heat. Fry tortilla pieces in hot oil until crisp. Drain on paper towels. Arrange pieces in a single layer on a cookie sheet.

Slice cheese into pieces which are the same size as the tortilla chips and cut the jalapeños in thin strips. Place one cheese slice on each tortilla piece and top with a jalapeño strip. Place under the broiler until the cheese is melted and bubbly. Serve at once.

YIELD: *2 dozen*

Panchos

A variation of Nachos, Panchos (as in Pancho Villa) are a spiffed-up version with the addition of refried beans and guacamole. There are many toppings which can be used. Try thinly sliced onions, a strip of grilled steak, a spoonful of chili, shredded chicken, or a spoonful of Picante Sauce (see Chapter 7) instead of the jalapeño. Flour tortillas can be used instead of corn tortillas.

6 corn tortillas
oil for frying
⅓ cup Refried Beans (Chapter 6)
¼ pound Monterrey Jack, Long-
horn, or Cheddar cheese, sliced

½ cup Guacamole (Chapter 3)
1 or 2 canned jalapeño peppers,
sliced

Quarter and fry tortillas as for Nachos. Spread refried beans on each tortilla chip and top with a cheese slice. Place under the broiler until the cheese melts. Remove and top each with a spoonful of guacamole and a jalapeño slice. Serve at once.

YIELD: *2 dozen*

Quesadillas

Our amigos from south of the border have given us many wonderful foods and food ideas. One of these is the Quesadilla (keh-sah-DEE-ya). It is a fried turnover made with masa harina (corn flour) which is filled with cheese and green chilies—not hot, only tasty.

1½ cups masa harina
¾ cup cold water
4 ounces Monterrey Jack cheese

¼ cup canned green chilies, chopped and drained
oil for frying

In a small bowl combine masa and water, mixing until the dough forms a ball. Add up to 3 tablespoons additional water if necessary. Divide the dough into 12 pieces and shape each into a 1½-inch ball. Cover the balls to prevent the dough from drying.

Place one ball between two sheets of plastic wrap. Flatten ball into a 4½-inch circle, using a rolling pin, the bottom of a pie plate, or a tortilla press. Carefully peel the tortilla from the plastic wrap and set aside. Continue with the remaining balls.

Cut the cheese into 12 thin strips. Place 1 cheese strip and 1 teaspoon chilies on one side of each of the circles. Fold over and press edges together to seal. If necessary, repair any breaks with fingers dipped in water. Repeat process until all 12 balls are done. Cover with a damp cloth until ready to fry.

Heat ½ inch oil in a small skillet over high heat. Fry each turnover, turning occasionally, until golden brown on both sides. Drain on paper towels and serve immediately.

YIELD: *1 dozen*

Tostados

Corn tortillas, when cut into pieces, fried until crisp, and then lightly salted are Tostados (tohs-TAH-dos) or homemade corn chips. Use them as the base for Nachos and Panchos, as you would any kind of chip for dips, as a garnish for Refried Beans (Chapter 6) or Guacamole (Chapter 3), or enjoy them by themselves or with some Fresh Mexican Salsa (Chapter 7). Delicioso!

12 corn or flour tortillas   **salt**
oil for frying

Cut tortillas in quarters. Heat 1 inch of oil in a small skillet over high heat. Fry tortilla pieces, 3 or 4 at a time, in hot oil until lightly golden and crisp. Drain on paper towels and lightly salt as desired.   YIELD: *4 dozen*

Jalapeño Cheese Pie

A subtle way of enjoying jalapeños is this Jalapeño Cheese Pie. It resembles a quiche without the crust and with just the fantastic flavor of the pepper. It is great for entertaining because it can be made ahead and refrigerated or frozen and simply heated before serving.

8–10 canned jalapeño peppers   **6 eggs, well beaten**
1 pound Cheddar cheese, grated

Cut jalapeños in half and rinse them under cool water, removing all seeds and membranes. Drain them well and chop finely.

Spread half of the grated cheese over the bottom of a 7-by-11-inch pan. Sprinkle the chopped jalapeños evenly over the cheese and top with the remaining cheese. Pour the beaten eggs over all.

Bake at 350° for 30–40 minutes or until the pie is set and slightly browned. Cool for 5–10 minutes and cut in bite-size squares for serving.   YIELD: *6 dozen*

Bean Rolls

Bean Rolls have few ingredients, are quick and easy to make, and are extremely good. Truly a South Texas favorite. Make plenty, because they go like hotcakes.

2 cups refried beans　　　　　**12 corn tortillas**
salt, pepper to taste　　　　　**oil for frying**

Heat refried beans, season as desired, and keep warm. Heat ½ inch oil in a small skillet over high heat. Using a pair of tongs, dip 1 tortilla at a time in hot oil for 1–2 seconds, only until softened.

Blot tortillas on paper towels to remove the excess oil. Place 2 heaping tablespoons of beans in a mound down the center of each tortilla. Roll in a cigar shape and serve immediately.

YIELD: *1 dozen*

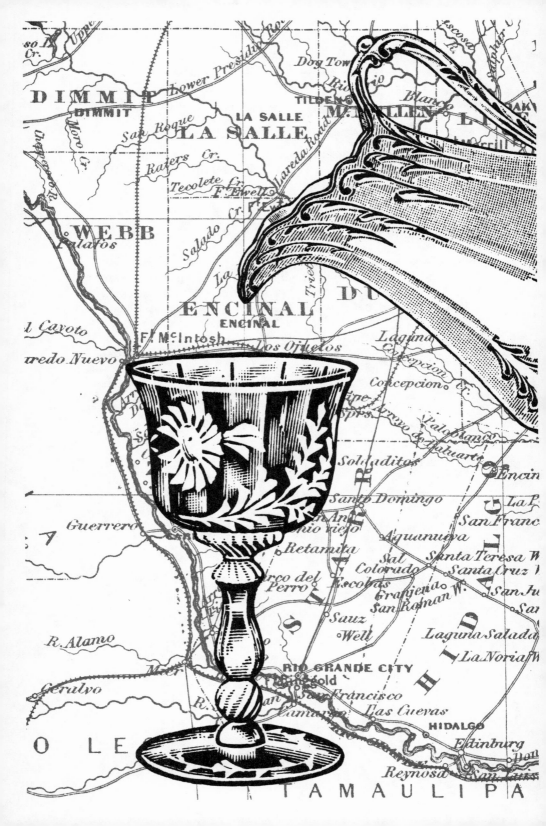

2. Drinks

Margaritas

Margaritas are probably the best-known tequila drink, and for a good reason: they are delicious. Many Texans entertain with a "Margarita party," where punch bowls are filled with the cool drink or it is served from pitchers garnished with lime slices and accompanied by a variety of Tex-Mex finger foods, such as Nachos, Panchos, Flaquitos, and Bean Rolls (see Chapter 1).

The Frozen Margarita is beautiful as well as good, especially when served in stemmed champagne-type glasses. The mixture resembles a smooth snow cone and mounds to a peak in the glass.

Although Margaritas taste like limeade, indulge with care or you may find yourself seeing pink armadillos.

1 ounce fresh lime juice	**4 ice cubes**
1½ ounces tequila	**½ fresh lime**
½ ounce Triple Sec	**salt**

Combine lime juice, tequila, Triple Sec, and ice in a cocktail shaker and shake until well blended and chilled.

Rub the rim of a champagne glass with lime half and dip in salt to coat.

Strain mixture into glass and serve.   YIELD: *1 serving*

Frozen Margaritas

6 ounces frozen limeade concentrate, undiluted
3 ounces Triple Sec
6 ounces tequila

2 cups crushed ice
½ fresh lime
salt

Combine limeade concentrate, Triple Sec, tequila, and ice in a
blender and blend until smooth.

Rub the rims of 6 champagne glasses with lime half and dip each
in salt to coat.

Pour frozen drinks into glasses and serve.

YIELD: *6 servings*

Tequila Sour

A take-off on the whiskey sour, a Tequila Sour is a refreshing
cocktail which is easy to prepare.

2 ounces lime juice
1½ ounces Simple Syrup (see
below)

3 ounces tequila
1 cup crushed ice
2 slices of lime (optional)

Mix all ingredients except lime slices in blender and strain into two
8-ounce sour glasses. Garnish with lime slices if desired.

YIELD: *2 servings*

SIMPLE SYRUP

1 cup water

1 cup sugar

Combine in saucepan, bring to a boil, and cook for 5 minutes. May
be stored in refrigerator for several weeks.

Tequila Solo

Tequila is Mexico's most popular drink and its popularity has crossed the Texas border. It is made from the juice of the agave plant and it packs quite a wallop.

Tequila is used as a base for many delicious mixed drinks, but the drinking of a "Solo" is steeped in tradition. To do it properly you must follow the ritual with the salt and the lime. Afterward, chase it with a cold beer, if desired, to help put out some of the fire.

1 jigger tequila   **shaker of salt**
wedge of lime

Assemble ingredients. Moisten the V between the thumb and index finger with tongue. Sprinkle salt on the moistened area. Take a bite of the lime pulp, lick the salt on the hand and down the jigger of tequila in one gulp. Chase with another bite of lime, if desired.   YIELD: *1 serving*

Desert Rose

The Desert Rose is a variation of the Solo and definitely not for the weak of heart. When the Tabasco is carefully added, a delicate rose-shape forms in the glass. Of course, the more of these you drink, the easier it is to see the "rose." But beware—the "rose" is the only thing that is delicate about this drink.

1 jigger tequila   **shaker of salt**
1 or 2 drops Tabasco sauce   **wedge of lime**

Gently add Tabasco sauce to tequila; watch as it forms a rose-shape in the glass. Then proceed as in Tequila Solo.

        YIELD: *1 serving*

Tequila Sunrise

This drink got its name from its different-colored layers, which resemble the sun as it begins to climb over the horizon.

5 ounces orange juice
2 ounces tequila
ice

1 ounce grenadine
sparkling water (optional)

In a cocktail shaker, combine orange juice, tequila, and ice and shake until well blended and chilled. Strain into a tall, ice-filled glass. Slowly add grenadine, allowing it to settle to the bottom, and serve with a straw.

Stir before drinking, adding a splash of sparkling water, if desired.   YIELD: *1 serving*

Laredo Gin Fizz

This drink originated in Nuevo Laredo, across the Mexican border from Laredo, Texas. After a long, hot day of shopping in the Mexican markets, you meander into a bar. The ceiling fans are humming overhead and the waiters are bustling around in their crisp white jackets. You feel cooler already. When you begin sipping this luscious, white, frothy drink, your feet don't hurt as much, your packages feel lighter, and you wonder why you didn't find this spot hours earlier.

However, you don't have to be in Laredo to enjoy all this. The effect is the same around the pool or patio. Just mix and serve in a tall glass with a straw; then sit back, relax, and let the "fizz" do the rest.

2 tablespoons powdered sugar
5–6 drops orange-flower water
1 tablespoon lime juice
1 tablespoon lemon juice

1½ ounces gin
1 egg white
2 tablespoons cream
½ cup crushed ice

Mix all ingredients in a blender. Pour into a tall glass and serve.
                                                   YIELD: *1 serving*

Sangrita

This cocktail will remind you of a Bloody Mary—until you taste it. *Grita* is Spanish for "scream," and, if you are not careful with the jalapeño liquid, you may do just that.

1½ cups tomato juice
¼ cup chopped onion
1 small clove garlic
1 teaspoon Worcestershire sauce

½ teaspoon salt
½–1 teaspoon liquid from canned jalapeños
3 ounces tequila

In a blender, combine tomato juice, onion, garlic, Worcestershire sauce, salt, and jalapeño liquid. Blend until smooth.

Strain and pour into ice-filled glasses. Add 1½ ounces tequila to each glass. Mix well and serve.   YIELD: *2 servings*

Sangria

Next to a cold beer, Sangria is probably the most popular Texas summertime beverage. To simply call it a wine punch would be to do a great injustice. The gorgeous color and the fruity flavors make it a delectable drink to accompany meals or to enjoy alone. Experiment by adding fresh fruits in season, such as strawberries or fresh pineapple. For a crowd, the recipe doubles, triples, or quadruples well and it looks as beautiful in a large punch bowl as it does in a clear pitcher.

2 oranges	**fifth of Burgundy**
1 lemon	**8–10 ounces club soda**
1 lime	**ice**
½ cup sugar	

Cut 1 orange, lemon, and lime into fourths. Squeeze juices from fruits into a pitcher and add the rinds and sugar. Stir with a wooden spoon to combine juice and sugar and press rinds with spoon to muddle. Add Burgundy and soda, mixing well. Pour into tall, ice-filled glasses. Slice the second orange and garnish each drink with an orange slice.   YIELD: *6 servings*

Red-Eye Special

Definitely the thing for "the morning after."

6 ounces tomato juice	**1 teaspoon Worcestershire sauce**
6 ounces beer	**Tabasco sauce (2–3 drops or to**
1 teaspoon lemon juice	**taste)**

Combine ingredients in a tall, ice-filled glass; stir and serve.
                                        YIELD: *1 serving*

Watermelon Punch

If you have ever sipped the juice which is left after eating a slice of watermelon, then you know the delicate flavor it has. Combined with lemonade, it is a refreshing drink on a hot afternoon. Add the vodka for a delightful party punch that is as pretty to look at as it is good to drink.

1 large watermelon
2 quarts lemonade
1 quart vodka

2 cups melon balls
crushed ice

Cut a thick slice off the top of the watermelon. Scoop out 2 cups of balls (or use a combination of cantaloupe, honeydew, and watermelon balls). Scoop out remaining meat and reserve. Refrigerate the shell and the balls.

Press the reserved watermelon meat through cheesecloth until you have 2 cups juice. Combine juice, lemonade, and vodka and chill well.

When ready to serve, place watermelon shell in crushed ice. Add vodka mixture, melon balls and ice.

YIELD: *28 4-ounce servings*

Coffee Liqueur

The thick, sweet Mexican coffee liqueur Kahlua is a wonderful after-dinner drink as well as a delicious "lace" for drinks such as Coffee Kahlua.

This is a recipe for a homemade version that tastes very much like the brand-name liqueur.

3 cups sugar
12 rounded teaspoons instant
   coffee (not freeze dried)

4 cups water
1 quart vodka
3 teaspoons vanilla

In a large saucepan combine sugar, coffee, and water. Bring to a boil, reduce heat, and simmer gently for 1 hour.

Cool coffee mixture and combine with vodka and vanilla. Pour
into a ½-gallon bottle and cork or seal tightly.

This liqueur can be used immediately and, if tightly sealed, will
keep indefinitely.   YIELD: *½ gallon*

Coffee Kahlua

4 cups black coffee
6 ounces Kahlua (or other coffee
** liqueur)**

6 tablespoons whipped cream
** (optional)**

To each cup of coffee, add 1½ ounces Kahlua and top with 1 tablespoon whipped cream, if desired.   YIELD: *4 servings*

Mexican Coffee

The blending of flavors of the coffee and the cinnamon make for an
aromatic as well as delicious brew. Sweetened with brown sugar or
perhaps a hint of Kahlua, Mexican Coffee is the perfect way to end
a meal. If desired, make it part of dessert by serving it with
Buñuelo Rosettes (Chapter 10).

6 tablespoons ground coffee
1 teaspoon ground cinnamon
4 cups water

8 cinnamon sticks
4 cups hot milk
brown sugar

Brew 6 tablespoons coffee with 1 teaspoon cinnamon, adding only 4
cups water, to make a strong coffee.

When ready to serve, place a cinnamon stick in each cup. Fill
half full with coffee. Add hot milk to fill, and sweeten as desired
with brown sugar. Stir with the cinnamon stick.

                                              YIELD: *8 servings*

Mexican Hot Chocolate

Mexican Hot Chocolate has a history dating back before the Spanish conquest. Today it is enjoyed by Texans and Mexicans alike for its delicious flavor and the fun of making it. There is a special Mexican chocolate made especially for this beverage which already has the sugar, cinnamon, and almond flavoring added, but the same results can be achieved by combining them yourself.

The fun comes in the beating. The children think of it as a game, so much so that there is a Mexican song just for the occasion: "Bate, bate el cho-co-la-te," meaning "beat, beat the chocolate." The beater which is traditionally used is called a *molinillo* and has a shape similar to a tom-tom stick. It is usually delicately carved and has wooden rings around the bottom which move freely to produce the foam. The *molinillo* is placed into the chocolate and the slender end is held between the palms of the hands. The beater is twirled by rubbing the palms together and thus beating the chocolate. The chocolate tastes just as good when made in a blender, but it is not as much fun.

The chocolate can be enjoyed any time a warm drink is called for, but it is a special treat at Christmastime, when it is traditionally served with Bizcochitos or Buñuelos (Chapter 10), perhaps after an evening of Christmas caroling.

2 ounces unsweetened chocolate	**pinch of salt**
2 tablespoons sugar	**4 cups milk**
1 teaspoon cinnamon	**dash of almond extract (optional)**

In the top of a double boiler, combine chocolate, sugar, cinnamon, salt, and 1 cup milk. Cook over medium heat until chocolate melts.

In a large saucepan, scald remaining 3 cups milk. Add chocolate mixture and almond extract, if desired, and blend well.

To serve, beat the chocolate with an electric or hand beater until foamy and pour into cups.   YIELD: *4 servings*

Spiced Tea

In Texas, when October and November roll around and the days begin to get shorter, we start looking forward with great anticipation to the first "norther" of the year—a cold front from the north which brings a welcome relief from the summer's heat and heralds the coming of fall/winter. As children, we could expect a big pot of Spiced Tea on the stove when we arrived home from school in celebration of this event or any time a good "warm-me-up" drink was called for.

Any leftover tea can be refrigerated and reheated for later use.

1 cup sugar	2½ cups pineapple juice
1 cup water	3 cups water
1 cinnamon stick	4 tea bags
2 lemons	1 quart hot water
2 oranges	

In a large pot, boil sugar, 1 cup water, and cinnamon stick for 5 minutes. To the sugar mixture, add the juice of the lemons and oranges (saving rinds) and the pineapple juice.

Cut up rinds of lemons and oranges. In a small saucepan, boil cut-up rinds in 3 cups water for 5 minutes. Add the 4 tea bags and allow to brew for 5 minutes. Strain this liquid into the juice mixture. Add 1 quart hot water. Bring entire mixture to a boil and simmer for 10 minutes. YIELD: *3 quarts*

Texas Sunshine

The Lower Río Grande Valley, at the southern tip of Texas between the Río Grande and the Gulf of Mexico, is a fertile region which is drenched with Texas sun and produces some of the best citrus fruit in the country. Texas Sunshine gives a taste of that special sun in liquid form. A "citrus-ade" concentrate, it can be made ahead and refrigerated, and it will be ready to mix and serve when needed. (If fresh mint is not available, it can be omitted.)

1½ cups sugar
2½ cups water
juice of 6 lemons

juice of 2 oranges
juice of 2 limes
1 cup fresh mint leaves

In a small saucepan, combine sugar and water and bring to a boil. Remove from heat and cool. Combine fruit juices and mint leaves. Pour cooled sugar syrup over juice mixture. Let stand for 1–2 hours. Strain and refrigerate.

When ready to serve, mix 1 part Texas Sunshine to 2 parts water or club soda. Pour over crushed ice and garnish with fruit or fresh mint leaves. YIELD: *1 quart concentrate or 3 quarts lemonade*

3. Soups and Salads

Avocado Soup

Guacamole is not the only way Texans enjoy avocados. When the big, luscious ones come in from Mexico, it is a good time for Avocado Soup. A cold soup, this thick, rich delicacy is just right as an appetizer for a summer luncheon, followed perhaps by Gulf Shrimp Salad. Garnish with a dollop of sour cream, a sprinkling of chopped watercress, a thin slice of cucumber, or a small spoonful of Picante Sauce (Chapter 7).

3 large ripe avocados
2–3 cups chicken stock
1 cup light cream
1 cup milk

1 teaspoon salt
¼ teaspoon onion salt
⅛ teaspoon fresh ground pepper
3–4 tablespoons lemon juice

Peel and seed avocados and puree in a food processor or blender, slowly adding 1 cup chicken stock, until smooth. Transfer to a large bowl.

Combine remaining stock, cream, and milk and gradually add to avocado mixture, beating with a wire whisk.

Stir in salt, onion salt, pepper, and lemon juice. Cover and refrigerate until well chilled.

To serve, check seasonings and thickness and add more milk or stock if needed.   YIELD: *6–8 servings*

Border Bean Soup

Hearty enough for a main course. Serve with a basket of hot Jalapeño Cornbread (Chapter 8).

½ pound bacon
2 onions, chopped
2 cloves garlic, minced
4 cups canned tomatoes with juice
6 cups cooked pinto beans

2 cups chicken stock or water
1 teaspoon vinegar
salt to taste
2 cups grated Longhorn or Cheddar cheese

In a large skillet, fry bacon; drain, crumble, and set aside, reserving drippings.

Sauté onions and garlic in bacon drippings (oil may be substituted) over medium heat until the onions are soft. Lower heat and add tomatoes, breaking them into small pieces. Simmer mixture for 10 minutes.

In a blender or food processor, puree cooked beans. Combine beans and chicken stock or water in a large pot and blend well. Stir in tomato mixture and vinegar and simmer over very low heat for 15–20 minutes. Add salt to taste.

To serve, ladle hot soup into bowls and top with grated cheese and crumbled bacon.   YIELD: *8–10 servings*

Bean Soup

The combination of two kinds of dried beans, a ham hock, and just a hint of jalapeño makes this soup a real winner. The aroma alone will have mouths watering.

1 cup dried navy beans
½ cup dried lima beans
4 quarts water
1 ham hock

1 carrot, thinly sliced
1 potato, cubed
1 canned or fresh jalapeño, minced

1½ cups canned tomatoes
1 large onion, chopped
¾ cup chopped celery
¼ cup chopped green pepper

¼ teaspoon basil
⅛ teaspoon marjoram
salt and pepper to taste

In a 6-quart pot, soak beans in 4 quarts water for several hours.
Add the ham hock and bring to a boil. Lower heat and simmer for
1 hour.

Add remaining ingredients and simmer for 3 hours.

YIELD: *12–16 servings*

Jack Cheese Soup

A surprisingly different cheese soup, smooth and delicious. It is
not for the weight-watcher but is just right for the first course on a
winter evening.

4 tablespoons butter
½ cup finely chopped onion
1 clove garlic, minced
4 tablespoons flour
2 cups milk
1 cup chicken stock

1 cup cream
2 cups grated Monterrey Jack
   cheese
⅓–½ cup canned green chilies,
   chopped

In a 2-quart saucepan, melt butter over medium heat and add
onion and garlic. Sauté until soft and transparent. Add flour and
blend until smooth. Combine milk and chicken stock. Slowly add to
flour mixture, stirring constantly, until thickened.

Lower heat and stir in cream. Add cheese gradually and continue cooking over low heat until melted. Do not let mixture boil.
Fold in green chilies and serve. YIELD: *4 servings*

Potato Soup

Potato Soup or, as our ancestors would say, Kartoffel Suppe is a rich, full-bodied soup of German origin. It makes a wonderful cold-weather luncheon or supper dish as well as a satisfying first course to a full dinner.

6 medium potatoes, peeled and quartered
2 medium onions
½ cup chopped celery
1 teaspoon salt
¼ teaspoon coarse ground black pepper

2 quarts water
2 tablespoons butter
½ cup cream
¼ cup chopped parsley
¼ teaspoon ground dill seed

In a large saucepan, combine potatoes, onions, celery, salt, pepper, and 2 quarts of water. Bring to a boil, cover, and simmer until potatoes are tender. Do not drain.

In a food processor or blender, puree vegetables with 2 cups liquid from pan. Slowly add pureed mixture to remaining liquid in pan, beating with a wire whisk, until smooth and well blended.

Stir in butter, cream, parsley, and dill. To serve, reheat over very low heat, being careful not to allow it to boil.

YIELD: *8–10 servings*

Ranch Hand Chicken Soup

When the hands came in for lunch after a morning on the range, a bowl of light chicken broth would never do the trick. This chicken soup is hearty and would take care of any size appetite. It was a favorite in the old days on the ranch or farm because whatever vegetables were in the garden or on hand could be used. And, indeed, any number of fresh or leftover vegetables still can be used. Just add any cooked vegetables when the tomatoes are added. Rice or cubed potatoes may be substituted for the noodles.

This is really a meal in a pot, so dish it up in big bowls and pass a basket of warm Jalapeño Cornbread (Chapter 8). If by chance you have any soup left over, it freezes well.

1 3½-pound chicken	1 cup fresh green beans, cut into
1 cup chopped celery	1-inch pieces
1 small onion, chopped	1 cup canned tomatoes with juice
1 zucchini squash, sliced	1–2 cups water
2 carrots, sliced	2 cups egg noodles
1 cup fresh or frozen peas	salt and pepper to taste

In a large pot, cook chicken in salted water, to cover, for 45–60 minutes or until chicken is tender.

Remove chicken, reserving broth. Allow chicken to cool. Remove skin and bone, and cut meat into bite-size pieces.

Bring stock to a slow boil and add fresh (or frozen) vegetables, cooking 15–20 minutes or until tender.

Add chicken meat, tomatoes (broken into pieces, if desired), and 1–2 cups water. Return soup to a boil and add noodles. Continue cooking until noodles are tender.

Season to taste and serve with hot Jalapeño Cornbread (Chapter 8).   YIELD: *8 servings*

Tortilla Soup

When you find a food you really like, you find as many ways to use it as possible. So it is with Texans and tortillas. Tortilla Soup is a light soup with a chicken stock base which works well as the first course to a Mexican dinner.

1 small onion, chopped	1 cup water
2 cloves garlic, pressed	1 teaspoon chili powder
2 tablespoons vegetable oil	1 teaspoon cumin (comino)
1 cup tomatoes, peeled and finely	salt to taste
chopped	4 corn tortillas, cut into 1-inch
3 cups chicken stock	pieces
1½ cups tomato juice	½ cup grated Cheddar cheese

In a 3- or 4-quart pan, sauté onions and garlic in oil until the onions are translucent. Add tomatoes, chicken stock, tomato juice, and water. Season with chili powder, cumin, and salt to taste. Cover and simmer 45–60 minutes.

Just before serving, bring liquid to a boil. Add tortillas and cheese. Cover, remove from heat, and let sit 3–5 minutes. Serve immediately.   YIELD: *6 servings*

Guacamole

To say that Guacamole is merely avocado salad would be an in-justice, for it is much more! Among other uses, it can be a dip with tostados or fresh vegetables, a topping for a Chalupa or Taco (see recipes in Chapters 4 and 5), or a garnish for Panchos (Chapter 1). Like many other Texas dishes, it can be made in a number of ways. Many people place the avocados in a blender or food pro-cessor instead of mashing them coarsely. Minced onions, chopped jalapeños, or chopped coriander can be added, or the tomato can be omitted. Regardless of how you prepare it or serve it, you'll enjoy it.

3 ripe avocados
2–3 tablespoons lemon or lime
   juice
1 large tomato, minced
½ teaspoon salt

½ teaspoon garlic powder or 1–2
   cloves garlic, pressed
1 tablespoon Picante Sauce
   (Chapter 7) (optional)

Peel and remove seeds from avocados and place the pulp on a large plate. Using a fork, coarsely mash the avocados until almost smooth. Drizzle with lemon or lime juice and add tomato, salt, garlic powder, and Picante Sauce (if desired). Mix well, cover with a piece of plastic wrap placed directly on top, and chill.

To serve as a salad, place a heaping tablespoonful on a lettuce leaf. Garnish with tostados, if desired.

YIELD: *6–8 salad servings*

Dad's Pea Salad

This was always our Dad's specialty salad, and all the children in the family loved it, even during our "salad-hating" stages. He had a tendency to change it around occasionally. When something interesting in the refrigerator caught his eye, he just threw it in. However, regardless of how differently it turned out, one thing remained the same: it was always delicious.

1 head lettuce	2 tablespoons white vinegar
2 large tomatoes	3 tablespoons cream
2 green onions	2 tablespoons juice from peas
2 stalks celery	½ teaspoon garlic powder
1 bell pepper	½ teaspoon salt
2 cups canned peas	1 teaspoon black pepper
1 cup mayonnaise	2–3 teaspoons sugar

Tear lettuce into bite-size pieces and place in a large salad bowl. Chop tomatoes, green onions, celery, and bell pepper into small pieces and add to lettuce. Drain peas, reserving liquid, and add to salad.

In a small bowl, combine remaining ingredients and stir until smooth.

Pour a generous amount of dressing over salad, toss thoroughly and serve immediately.   YIELD: *8 servings*

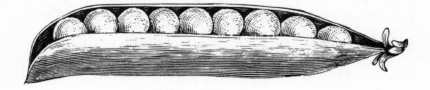

Gulf Shrimp Salad

Shrimp salad is a luncheon favorite everywhere. Texans think that the delicious shrimp from the Gulf of Mexico add a special flavor, and this version of the salad will hit the spot when the mercury begins to soar.

3 cups shredded iceberg lettuce	1 cup mayonnaise
2 tomatoes, chopped	3 tablespoons white vinegar
2 stalks celery, chopped	3 tablespoons cream
½ cup chopped onion	2 tablespoons lemon juice
½ pound cooked shrimp, cut into	½ teaspoon salt
small pieces	½–1 teaspoon black pepper
3 hard-boiled eggs, sliced	1 teaspoon sugar

Combine lettuce, tomatoes, celery, and onion in a salad bowl. Add the shrimp pieces and the hard-boiled eggs, reserving several egg slices for garnish.

For the dressing, combine the remaining ingredients and mix until smooth.

Pour a generous amount of dressing over the salad and toss well. Garnish with the reserved egg slices and serve immediately.   YIELD: *4 servings*

Sour Cream Cucumbers

Always a family favorite for Sunday dinner, Sour Cream Cucumbers are an excellent side dish or salad. The onions and cucumbers are crisp, and their flavors meld deliciously with the sour cream dressing. For a variation add some snipped fresh dill.

3 large cucumbers, peeled and	½ cup white vinegar
sliced	1 teaspoon salt
1 onion, thinly sliced	pepper to taste
1 cup sour cream	½ teaspoon sugar

Layer cucumbers and onion slices, separated into rings, alternately in a glass or ceramic bowl.

Combine sour cream, vinegar, salt, pepper, and sugar. Stir until blended and smooth. Pour over cucumbers and onion rings.

Cover and refrigerate 4–6 hours or overnight, tossing once or twice. YIELD: *4–6 servings*

Marinated Black-Eyed Peas

About seventy-five miles southeast of Dallas lies the small town of Athens, Texas, where the best black-eyed peas around are grown. In July, when the peas reach perfection, the people of Athens hold their annual celebration, the Black-eyed Pea Jamboree. This is a good time to make up a batch of Marinated Black-eyed Peas—some to enjoy right away and some to put away for later. They make a delightful change-of-pace summer salad and a savory condiment on into fall and winter.

2 cups shelled black-eyed peas	**1 teaspoon salt**
1 cup vegetable oil	**ground pepper to taste**
⅓ cup wine vinegar	**1 tablespoon minced parsley**
1 (whole) clove garlic	**1 small onion, thinly sliced**

In a medium saucepan, cover shelled peas with salted water. Bring to a boil, then simmer for 30–40 minutes or until peas are tender, but firm.

Prepare marinade while peas are cooking. Combine oil, vinegar, garlic clove, salt, pepper, and parsley.

When peas are done, drain and toss, while warm, with sliced onion. Pour marinade over both.

Refrigerate for at least 2 days and up to 2 weeks. Remove garlic clove after the first day. Drain before serving.

YIELD: *4 salad servings or
6–8 condiment servings*

Cole Slaw

Salt and pepper, pretzels and beer, baseball games and hot dogs—some things just go together. So it is that when we fry up a big batch of fish we also make a big bowl of cole slaw. But don't wait for a fish fry to make this salad because it's a good partner for barbecue or fried chicken as well.

4 cups shredded cabbage	½ teaspoon sugar
1 cup grated carrots	1 tablespoon cider vinegar
½ cup chopped green bell pepper	1 tablespoon lemon juice
⅔ cup mayonnaise	1 tablespoon milk
¼ teaspoon salt	dash Tabasco sauce
pepper to taste	¼ cup chopped green onion

Combine cabbage, carrots, and green pepper and toss to mix well. Combine remaining ingredients and pour over cabbage mixture. Toss and refrigerate until ready to serve. Toss well before serving.   YIELD: *4–6 servings*

Sauerkraut Salad

As we are of strong German stock, sauerkraut was often served in our home. All of the children loved it, especially our younger brother who, unable to pronounce it, called it "salad kraut." This recipe could have been inspired by a similar mistake made by an earlier child. It is a crisp, colorful salad that is perfect picnic fare. Make it in a large glass jar and it will be ready to pop into the picnic basket.

1½ cups sugar	2 large carrots, grated
¾ cup vinegar	1 green bell pepper, finely
2 cups chopped celery	chopped
1 cup chopped onion	3 cups sauerkraut, drained

In a saucepan, combine sugar and vinegar and bring to a boil. Allow to cool.

Combine vegetables and sauerkraut in a large salad bowl. Pour cooled sugar mixture over all and toss to distribute. Cover and refrigerate overnight or for up to 3 days.

YIELD: *10–12 servings*

Taco Salad

When it's just too hot to stay in the kitchen and fry taco shells and everyone is really "taco hungry," Taco Salad is the answer. It has the wonderful flavor of a taco with all the trimmings in a cool and satisfying salad form. Serve with Picante Sauce (Chapter 7) if desired.

1 pound ground beef
½ teaspoon garlic salt
1 head lettuce
½ cup chopped onion
1 cup grated Cheddar cheese
1 medium tomato, chopped
1 cup Ranch Dressing (Chapter 7)

2 cups corn chips or Tostados (Chapter 1)
1 avocado, sliced (optional)
chopped canned jalapeños to taste (optional)
black olives to taste (optional)

Brown ground beef and season with garlic salt. Drain on paper towels and set aside.

Tear lettuce into bite-size pieces and place in a large bowl. Add onion, cheese, tomato, and ground beef and toss to mix well. Add dressing and toss until lettuce is well coated.

Just before serving, add chips or Tostados and avocado, jalapeños, and/or black olives as desired, and toss lightly. Serve immediately.

YIELD: *4–6 servings*

White Sand Hills
Ellis Waterhole
Sierra Pancut
Ft. Davis
San Esteram
Alamo

4. Meats

Texas Hofbrau Steak

The word *hofbrau* comes from Germany. Originally, each brewery had its own garden or terrace on the grounds where the brew could be sampled and enjoyed. It was by no means a "beer joint," but more of a family spot and a cultural meeting place. These gardens came to be known as Hof (garden or terrace) Brau (a shortened word for brewery).

The word has evolved through the years and now it is the symbol for a popular meeting place where good food and cold beer are served.

One favorite item from a Hofbrau menu is this sirloin steak. For real authenticity, serve it with Grilled Onions and Ranch Fried Potatoes (see Chapter 6 for recipes).

2 pounds sirloin steak, ½ inch thick
4 tablespoons margarine

½ cup lemon juice
¾ cup margarine
4 teaspoons garlic salt

Cut steak into serving-size pieces. Heat 4 tablespoons margarine in a frying pan over high heat.

Pan-fry steak pieces in the margarine, 2–3 minutes per side. When all pieces have been fried, add remaining ingredients to pan and heat until margarine is melted.

Pour a generous serving of sauce over each steak.

YIELD: *4–6 servings*

Smothered Steak

A real down-home dish, Smothered Steak is steak and onions smothered in a thick, delicious gravy. It is easy to prepare because the gravy makes itself as the steak and onions cook.

2 pounds round steak
1 cup flour
1 teaspoon salt
½ teaspoon pepper

¼ cup oil (or more) for frying
2 medium onions, sliced
3 cups water

Trim steak and cut into serving-size pieces. Pound with a meat mallet or the edge of a saucer to tenderize.

Combine flour, salt, and pepper. Dredge each piece of meat in the flour mixture, using the mallet or plate.

Heat ¼ cup oil in a large skillet over high heat. Brown each piece of steak in the hot oil, setting aside when browned. Add more oil if necessary. When all meat has been browned, add sliced onions to the pan, separating as you add them. Cook only until soft and remove from skillet.

Lower heat to medium and return meat pieces layered with onions to skillet. Add water and cover. Cook over medium heat until steak is tender and gravy has thickened, about 30–45 minutes.   YIELD: *4–6 servings*

Chicken-Fried Steak

Bring a big appetite when you are ready for this dish because eating Chicken-Fried Steak Texas style is an event. The rules are easy to follow: (1) You eat it covered with Cream Gravy (Chapter 7). (2) There must be plenty of mashed potatoes and gravy on the side. (3) A basket of hot biscuits should be passed around at least twice. (4) You clean your plate. (5) You sit back and loosen your belt buckle. (6) You never feel guilty about how much you ate. Everyone deserves a good Chicken-Fried Steak dinner every once in a while!

1 pound round steak or minute
  steak
1 cup flour
1 teaspoon salt

½ teaspoon pepper
oil for frying
½ cup evaporated milk

Cut steak into 4 pieces and pound to tenderize, if necessary. Combine flour, salt, and pepper.

In a heavy skillet, heat ¼ inch oil. Dip each piece of steak in flour mixture, then into evaporated milk and into flour mixture again. Fry in oil over medium-high heat until lightly browned. Remove and drain on paper towels.   YIELD: *4 servings*

Brisket in Beer

A brisket is likely the most popular cut of beef for Texas Style Barbecue (see the following recipe). But, if you don't feel like tending the fire, try Brisket in Beer. It is excellent party fare because you can put it on the night before and let it cook all night. When you wake up in the morning, you will find a beautifully browned piece of beef in a delicious pan gravy.

To serve, simply reheat the brisket and cut it into wafer-thin slices against the grain. Arrange the slices on a serving platter and drizzle a little pan gravy over the top. Have a basket of small, split rolls alongside and a bowl of the remaining pan gravy. A relish tray and some assorted cheeses could round out your table, and you can step back and enjoy your own party.

3–4 pounds beef brisket
1 teaspoon salt

½ teaspoon pepper
2 12-ounce cans beer

Season brisket with salt and pepper and place in a roasting pan. Pour beer around brisket and cover the pan tightly with aluminum foil. Bake at 325° 6–8 hours or overnight.

Remove meat and strain off grease from the pan. Add enough water or beer to the pan drippings to make a rich gravy.

Cut the meat in thin slices, against the grain, and serve with the pan gravy.   YIELD: *6–8 servings*

Texas Style Barbecue

Barbecue is an integral part of Texas life. The word refers not only to food, but to an event. The invitation "Come over, we're having a barbecue" epitomizes the casual, warm atmosphere of an occasion which lends itself to family, friends, and good times.

There are probably as many different ways and ideas of barbecuing in the state as there are ways to cook chili or a pot of beans, or even to spell *barbecue*. Whether you are down at the farm in the shade of an oak tree with tables spread with checkered cloths or in your own back yard, the main thing to remember is that it should be an enjoyable, relaxed time for all involved, including the chef. We hope the following tips will help to make it so.

Happy Barbecue, Bar-B-Que, Bar-B-Q, Bar-B-Cue, Barbecuing, Barbeque, etc.!

Preparing the Coals: Build a fire with oak, mesquite, hickory wood, or charcoal briquets. Do not start cooking until the flames die down and the coals are grey or white at the top and glowing red on the inside. It will take 20–30 minutes to get the coals to this point. When coals are ready, distribute them evenly for uniform cooking.

Adjusting the Grill: Different meats must be cooked at various distances from the coals for best results. Check the recipe and follow the instructions carefully.

Covering the Grill: Closing the lid or covering enhances the smoke flavor in the meat and also makes for more even cooking. However, check the fire frequently to make sure it does not go out.

Basting: Basting is essential to good barbecue. It keeps the meat moist and juicy. However, a sauce made with tomatoes or any form of sugar will burn quickly and leave a bitter taste. For best results, use Basting Sauce for Barbecue (Chapter 7) for basting while cooking meat. Baste with a pastry brush or paint brush. If a tomato-base sauce or sweet sauce is desired, brush on 2–3 minutes before meat is ready to be taken off the grill. Serve the remaining sauce along with the barbecue.

Minding the Meat: Check on the barbecue at 20–30 minute intervals. It will probably need turning or basting, and you should also make sure the fire is still in good shape.

In addition to the barbecue recipes in this chapter, see Barbecued Chicken Texas Style and Barbecued Quail with Bacon in Chapter 5. For sauce recipes, see Chapter 7.

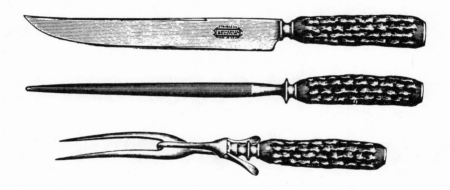

Barbecued Brisket

9–12 pound beef brisket
10–15 garlic cloves (optional)
salt and pepper to taste

Basting Sauce for Barbeuce
(Chapter 7)

Trim brisket of any excess fat, rinse with cold water, and pat dry. If desired, make 10–30 holes in the brisket and stuff a whole or halved garlic clove in each. Season with salt and pepper, as desired.

Prepare coals and position grill 8 inches above them. Place prepared brisket on grill and cook very slowly for 4–5 hours, with grill covered. Turn and baste every 20–30 minutes.

Remove from grill and serve when brisket is evenly browned and tender.

YIELD: *12 servings*

Barbecued Beef Ribs

10–12 pounds beef short ribs
seasonings to taste

Basting Sauce for Barbecue
(Chapter 7)

Follow directions for Barbecued Brisket, but decrease cooking time to 2½–3 hours.   YIELD: *8 servings*

Barbecued Spareribs

8 pounds fresh pork ribs
seasonings to taste

Basting Sauce for Barbecue
(Chapter 7)

Cut spareribs into serving-size pieces, if desired. Follow directions for Barbecued Brisket, but decrease cooking time to 1½–2 hours.   YIELD: *6–8 servings*

South Texas Steak

The marinade makes this grilled steak extra special. For a great barbecue menu, try this steak with Chili-Cheese Casserole, Roasted Corn (see Chapter 6 for recipes), and a fresh green salad.

4 pounds sirloin steak, 1–1½
**   inches thick**
½ cup red wine vinegar
½ cup brown sugar
3 tablespoons catsup

3 tablespoons Worcestershire
**   sauce**
1 tablespoon prepared mustard
1 clove garlic, crushed

Trim steak, cut into 8 pieces, and place in a nonmetallic dish. Combine remaining ingredients and pour over meat. Marinate for at least 2 hours or overnight.

Grill over hot coals, 4 to 6 inches from heat, basting with marinade, 6–8 minutes per side for medium rare or 8–10 minutes per side for medium. Heat remaining marinade and serve with steak.
                    YIELD: *8 servings*

Anacuchos

Texas won its independence from Mexico at the Battle of San Jacinto on April 21, 1836. This date is celebrated state-wide, and especially in San Antonio, where the week which includes April 21 is set aside each year for a city-wide celebration—Fiesta. The word itself means "party" in Spanish, and that is exactly what happens. There are parades, including one on the San Antonio River, fairs, carnivals, exhibits, band contests, and fireworks displays.

One of the most popular events during the entire week is "A Night in Old San Antonio." It is held in historic La Villita (Little Village), which was the original downtown area of San Antonio over 150 years ago. Foods, drinks, games, music, and dancing of all kinds are there.

Out of all of the food choices, there is one distinct favorite—the Anacuchos. On sight they look like a regular shishkebab, but the first bite will tell you that they are something more.

1 cup red wine vinegar
1 cup water
1½ teaspoons salt
1 teaspoon whole peppercorns
2 fresh Serrano chilies
1 clove garlic
pinch of oregano

pinch of ground cumin (comino)
2½ pounds beef, cut into 1½-inch cubes
2½ pounds pork, cut into 1½-inch cubes
oil for basting

Place all ingredients except meat and oil in a blender and process until they are well mixed.

Pour marinade over meat in a glass or ceramic bowl. Cover and refrigerate for 24–48 hours.

Thread wooden skewers with 5 or 6 pieces of meat each (alternating beef and pork). Brush with oil and grill over very hot coals, 4–6 inches from heat, about 2 minutes per side. Be careful not to overcook. Baste with marinade just before serving.

YIELD: *8–10 servings*

Homestead Hash

One of the best things about the traditional Sunday roast was always the Monday night hash. Don't write it off as just another leftover dish—it is much too good.

3 cups cooked beef, cubed	salt and pepper to taste
3 large poatoes, peeled and cubed	2 tablespoons cornstarch
1 medium onion, chopped	¼ cup water
3 tablespoons vegetable oil	
2 cups beef stock, or mixture of pan drippings and water	

In a large, heavy skillet, sauté beef, potatoes, and onion in oil over medium heat until well browned. Add stock or pan drippings and season to taste. Cover and simmer over low heat until potatoes are tender—15–20 minutes.

Combine cornstarch and water to make a smooth paste. Slowly add to meat mixture, stirring constantly, until thickened.

YIELD: *4–6 servings*

Beef Jerky

A staple in the saddlebags of any cowboy, jerky is still a Texas tradition. As we were growing up, the smell of the smoke from Grandpa's smokehouse never ceased to make our mouths water, and we couldn't wait for the day when he would pronounce the jerky ready. Unfortunately, not many of us have a smokehouse out back, but this oven version is the next best thing. The jerky makes a super snack and is a welcome treat in a lunch box.

2 pounds round steak	2 teaspoons garlic salt
3 tablespoons natural smoke flavoring (optional)	2 teaspoons black pepper
3 tablespoons Worcestershire sauce	

Cut meat into very thin strips ¾ inch wide and 3–4 inches long; place in mixing bowl.

Mix the other ingredients and pour over meat strips, mixing thoroughly. Set aside for 15–30 minutes. Place foil in bottom of oven to catch drippings. Using small wood or bamboo sticks, skewer each piece of meat through one end. Place sticks crosswise on oven rack, allowing meat to hang through rungs of rack.

Turn oven to lowest setting (or about 120°) and oven-cure meat 8–10 hours, leaving the oven door open no more than ½ inch.

When completly dried, the strips will keep in closed jars for up to 3 months.   YIELD: *4–5 dozen strips*

Ground Beef Stew

This is a delicious and different twist to an old favorite. You can personalize it by adding a variety of ingredients, but you will love it as is. Try putting it on in the morning in a slow cooker (putting all the ingredients in at once) and come home that evening to a hearty one-dish meal.

6 slices bacon
1 cup chopped onion
½ cup chopped green bell pepper
2 cloves garlic, minced
1½ pounds ground beef
12 tomatoes peeled and diced,
    with their juice

1 cup water
1 teaspoon salt
pepper to taste
1 tablespoon chili powder
1 cup cooked corn
1 cup cooked pinto beans
2 cups cubed potatoes (peeled)

In a large pan or Dutch oven, fry bacon until crisp. Drain on paper towels and set aside. Sauté onion, green pepper, and garlic in the bacon drippings (or oil may be substituted) over medium heat. Add the ground beef and cook until browned. Lower the heat and add the tomatoes (with their juice), water, salt, pepper, and chili powder. Cover and cook slowly for 30 minutes.

Add corn, beans, and poatoes and continue cooking for 20 minutes or until the potatoes are tender.

When ready to serve, crumble bacon and sprinkle over the stew.   YIELD: *8 servings*

Chuckwagon Stew

When the dogies were asleep and the dust had settled on the range, many a cowpoke would settle around the campfire with a cup of hot coffee, a big plate of stew, and some hot biscuits to sop up the gravy. The cook never made the stew the same way twice, having to improvise with what happened to be on hand. Likewise, you can just use this recipe as a basis and go on from there.

1 cup chopped onion
1 clove garlic, minced
2 tablespoons bacon drippings or
  vegetable oil
2 pounds beef stew meat, cut into
  1½-inch cubes
½ cup flour
salt and pepper to taste
2½ cups beef stock

1 teaspoon salt
½ teaspoon pepper
1 tablespoon Worcestershire
  sauce
6 small carrots, peeled
4 medium potatoes, peeled
1 tablespoon flour
¼ cup water

In a large pot or Dutch oven, sauté onions and garlic in bacon drippings or oil. Dredge beef cubes in ½ cup flour seasoned with salt and pepper and brown with onions and garlic.

Add stock, 1 teaspoon salt, ½ teaspoon pepper, and Worcestershire sauce and bring to a boil. Cover and simmer for 1 hour.

Cut carrots into 1–2-inch slices and cube potatoes. Add to beef mixture and simmer an additional 30 minutes or until vegetables are tender.

Combine 1 tablespoon flour with ¼ cup water to make a paste. Gradually stir into stew and cook until sauce has thickened.

YIELD: *4–6 servings*

Aunt Jackie's Beer Stew

Even Texans who don't drink beer cook with it, for they know the wonderful flavor it imparts. The beer makes this stew a special dish and moves it from family fare to party fare. Serve it over rice or egg noodles with a green salad and plenty of crusty French bread.

1 medium onion, chopped
1 pound mushrooms, sliced
6 tablespoons butter
3 pounds lean stew meat
1½ tablespoons flour
1 tablespoon brown sugar
2 teaspoons dry mustard
¾ cup tomato paste

¼ cup chopped parsley
2 tablespoons whole peppercorns
2 bay leaves
½ teaspoon salt
pinch of thyme
1 clove garlic, crushed
2 12-ounce cans beer

Sauté onion and mushrooms in butter in a large pan or Dutch oven. Add the stew meat and continue cooking until browned. Sprinkle flour, brown sugar, and dry mustard over beef. Add remaining ingredients and mix well. Cover and let simmer for 1½–2 hours or until beef is tender.   YIELD: *8 servings*

Tacos

If there is one food that is a staple for most Texans, it would be the taco. Because of this, the methods of preparing and the variety of fillings are endless! (In addition to those given here, see Chicken Taco Filling in Chapter 5.)

A basic taco is a corn or flour tortilla fried in a U-shape.

To prepare, heat ½ inch oil in a small skillet. Using tongs, immerse half of the tortilla in the hot oil and fry until just crisp. Roll the other half into the oil and fry. Use tongs to hold the top edges apart so there will be a 1–1½-inch opening. Drain on paper towels and fill as desired. The filling may be topped with lettuce, tomatoes, onions, grated cheese, and hot sauce, if desired.

Beef Taco Filling

1½ pounds ground meat
1 teaspoon salt
1½ tablespoons flour
1½ tablespoons chili powder

1½ cups water
½ teaspoon cumin (comino)
½ teaspoon garlic powder

In a skillet, sauté ground meat until brown and crumbly; drain grease.

Combine salt, flour, and chili powder and sprinkle over meat, stirring to distribute evenly. Add water, cumin, and garlic powder. Continue cooking over medium heat until thickened. Stir occasionally to prevent sticking.   YIELD: *filling for 12–14 tacos*

Salpicón

Salpicón is a flavorful shredded meat dish which is primarily used as a filling for flour tortilla Tacos or Burritos or as a tasty topping for Panchos or Nachos (Chapter 1).

Leftover roast can be used if it is not too dry.

2½–3 pounds chuck or shoulder
  roast
¼ cup oil or lard
1 onion, quartered and thinly
  sliced

2 cloves garlic, minced
salt to taste

Cover roast with water in a Dutch oven and bring to a boil. Cover, lower heat, and simmer 1½–2 hours, or until meat is tender and beginning to fall off bone. Allow beef to cool in broth until it is cool enough to handle.

Remove beef and drain. Using your hands or two forks, finely shred the beef and set aside.

In a large skillet, heat oil or lard. Sauté onion and garlic until soft. Add the beef and cook over medium high heat until browned and crisp on edges. Add more oil if necessary. Season with salt to taste.   YIELD: *10–12 servings*

Texas Special

A different kind of taco filling, Texas Special is a handy recipe that is equally good with flour tortillas, as here, or in a fried Taco, in a Burrito, or on a Chalupa, topped with Picante Sauce, of course.

1 pound ground beef
1 medium onion, finely chopped
1 cup cooked spinach, chopped
1–2 teaspoons salt

2 eggs, well beaten
8 flour tortillas, warmed
1 cup grated Monterrey Jack
  cheese

In a large skillet, brown beef and onion. Stir in cooked spinach and salt and simmer over medium heat for 5–10 minutes. Add beaten eggs and stir fry with a fork until eggs are set.

To serve, placed a large spooonful of meat mixture on a warm tortilla. Top with a sprinkling of grated cheese and fold in half to close.   YIELD: *4 servings*

Fajitas

Fajitas are perhaps the ultimate taco filling. To make them, a marinated skirt steak is grilled and then sliced into thin cross-grain strips. Some aficionados say that authentic Fajitas must be grilled over a mesquite fire, but they are delectable regardless of the type of fire used as long as they are not overcooked.

We cannot deny, though, that being out in the wide open spaces under the stars around a pit fire of mesquite, its distinctive aroma filling the air and fajitas grilling, is a scenario beyond compare. But in this case, perhaps it is the atmosphere as well as the mesquite which prompts such absolutes!

Fajitas can be prepared in a variety of ways. The recipe below features a more elaborate marinade. However, the steaks can be marinated or simply brushed and basted with a preparation of ¾ cup fresh lime juice, 2 large cloves of garlic, pressed, and ¼ cup oil to each 2½–3 pounds of meat. This variation produces delicious results.

1 cup dry red wine	½ teaspoon basil
½ cup oil	1 teaspoon whole peppercorns
½ cup red wine vinegar	2½ pounds skirt steak
2 tablespoons Worcestershire	12 flour tortillas
sauce	Fresh Mexican Salsa (Chapter 7)
2 cloves garlic	1 onion, thinly sliced
1 teaspoon oregano	

Combine wine, oil, vinegar, Worcestershire sauce, garlic, oregano, basil, and peppercorns in a large, nonmetallic bowl. Add steak and toss well. Marinate 24–48 hours in the refrigerator. Toss several times during marination.

Grill steaks over a very hot fire, 4–6 inches from heat, 3–4 minutes per side. Do not overcook.

Cut steaks in thin strips across the grain. Warm tortillas.

To serve, place a portion of the meat strips down the center of each tortilla. Top with salsa and sliced onions and fold in half or overlap the edges.   YIELD: *4–6 servings*

Beef Enchiladas

The endless variations of enchiladas account for the fact that few Mexican or Tex-Mex dishes can rival this one in popularity. The Tex-Mex version consists of corn tortillas wrapped around a filling, placed in a casserole, and topped with a sauce.

Most Texans prefer Beef Enchiladas, but Cheese Enchiladas are a favorite as well. To prepare these, omit the beef and double the amount of cheese. Use half of the cheese as the filling and continue as directed for Beef Enchiladas.

From here, only your imagination can limit you, as enchiladas are as versatile as crepes or pasta.

1 pound ground beef	oil for frying
3 tablespoons oil	12 corn tortillas
2 tablespoons flour	1 pound Longhorn or Cheddar
1–2 tablespoons chili powder	cheese, grated
2 cups water	1 onion, finely chopped (optional)
½ teaspoon salt	

Brown ground beef and set aside. In a large skillet, combine 3 tablespoons oil and the flour and cook over medium heat until flour begins to brown. Add chili powder to water and stir until dissolved. When flour is browned, slowly add chili powder mixture, stirring constantly, until it begins to thicken. Add salt, lower heat, and simmer uncovered for 5–10 minutes.

Heat ½ inch oil in a small skillet. Dip each tortilla in hot oil to soften.

To assemble enchiladas, place 2 tablespoons ground beef, some grated cheese, and chopped onion (if desired) along the middle of a softened tortilla. Roll up and place, seam side down, in a 9-by-13-inch casserole. Repeat process with the remaining tortillas. Pour sauce over the top and sprinkle with the remaining cheese and chopped onion.

Bake at 350° about 15 minutes or until enchiladas are heated through and cheese has melted. YIELD: *6 servings*

Burritos

A Burrito is a large, thin flour tortilla which can be filled with many different fillings.

To prepare, make Flour Tortillas (Chapter 8), rolling dough into circles about 10 inches in diameter.

Spread Refried Beans (Chapter 6) on each warm tortilla and place several spoons of filling down the center. Fold up 2 inches of the bottom edge of the tortilla. Then roll the sides of the tortilla into a tube shape.

Use Carne con Chiles, Salpicón, or Huevos con Chorizo (Chapter 5) for the filling. Serve with Hot Sauce (Chapter 7), if desired.

Burritos make great lunch box treats and can be frozen when a meat filling is used.

Beef Chalupas

A chalupa is the Tex-Mex counterpart of an open-faced sandwich. A fried tortilla (corn or flour) is the base, and there the rules end, for the toppings, as with taco fillings, can be as varied as those for a sandwich.

The most common version is a fried corn tortilla topped with refried beans, ground beef, grated cheese, lettuce, tomato, onion, and hot sauce. But do not stop there! Flour tortillas are equally tasty as a base, and any taco filling can double as a chalupa topping. (See also Chicken Chalupas, Chapter 5.)

12 corn tortillas
oil for frying
1 pound ground beef
salt to taste
2 cups Refried Beans (Chapter 6)
2 cups grated Longhorn or
　Cheddar cheese

3 cups shredded lettuce
1½ chopped tomato
1 cup chopped onion
Picante Sauce (Chapter 7)
　(optional)

In a small frying pan, heat ½ inch oil over high heat. Fry tortillas, one at a time, until crisp. Drain on paper towels.

Sauté ground beef, seasoned with salt to taste, until browned. Heat refried beans.

To assemble chalupas, spread a portion of beans on the fried tortilla, top with some ground beef, sprinkle with cheese, and top with lettuce, tomato, and onion. Spoon on Picante Sauce if desired.

YIELD: *6 servings*

Tortilla Casserole

A delicious and different casserole that has just a hint of Mexican flavor, this is a make-ahead dish that assures easy entertaining. (It can be cooked immediately but is better if refrigerated overnight.) Make several and put one in the freezer for a great dinner any time. (The recipe may be doubled for a 9-by-13-inch casserole.)

1 pound ground beef
½ cup chopped onion
1 clove garlic, minced
3 large tomatoes, peeled and
  chopped
1 cup cooked spinach, drained
  and chopped
salt and pepper to taste
1½ cups sour cream

¾ cup evaporated milk
½ teaspoon garlic powder
4–6 tablespoons melted butter
6–8 corn tortillas
⅓ cup canned green chilies,
  chopped
2 cups grated Longhorn or
  Cheddar Cheese

In a large skillet, brown ground beef, onions, and garlic, and drain off any grease. Add chopped tomatoes (with juices), spinach, and salt and pepper.

In a small bowl, combine sour cream, evaporated milk, and garlic powder and mix until well blended and smooth.

Dip tortillas in melted butter. Place half the tortillas in a layer on the bottom and sides of a shallow 1½-quart casserole dish. Spread meat mixture over tortillas. Sprinkle green chilies and 1½ cups grated cheese over meat. Pour half of the sour cream mixture over the cheese. Cut remaining tortillas into 1½-inch strips and layer them over the cream mixture. Top tortillas with remaining cream mixture and sprinkle with remaining ½ cup cheese.

Refrigerate overnight or freeze for up to 2 months. Bake at 350° 30–40 minutes (60–75 minutes if frozen) or until cheese is melted and mixture is heated through.   YIELD: *4 servings*

Chili

A statewide favorite and a dish that is synonymous with Texas is chili. However, Texans have never agreed on the best way to make a "bowl of red" and probably never will. According to our grandmother, chili was first prepared on Military Plaza in downtown San Antonio around 1872. There the "chili queens" would spread their long tables with oilcloths and dish up their famous chili twenty-four hours a day for the trail riders who would come into town.

The chili recipes that follow are all different, mainly because as the recipes were passed along, each cook added his or her own touch. There is not a chili-cooking person in Texas who does not think that he or she makes the best chili around; the many chili cooking contests all over the state are proof of this. From the small "Chili Cook-Off" at a county fair to the "World Championship" in Terlingua, chili lovers from all over vie for the coveted prize using a variety of ingredients: armadillo meat, rattlesnake, venison, beef, tomatoes, beans, beer, peppers, or a "secret" ingredient.

Texans' passion for chili lives on. In the next 100 years there will probably continue to be discussions on what ingredients belong in chili. One thing is sure: there can be no right or wrong recipe, only one that tastes best to you. Enjoy a big bowl with some hot cornbread, saltine crackers, or a soft, warm tortilla and experience a real taste of Texas.

Basic Chili

2 pounds chili meat (very coarse
   ground beef)
1 large onion, chopped
2 cloves garlic, minced
2 tablespoons oil
2 teaspoons ground cumin
   (comino)

1 tablespoon chili powder
salt and pepper to taste
3 cups canned tomatoes with
   juice
1 cup water

In a large pot, sauté meat, onion, and garlic in oil over medium heat until browned. Stir in cumin, chili powder, salt, and pepper. Add tomatoes, breaking them up into small pieces as you add them. Add water and mix well.

Simmer over low heat, uncovered, for 1–2 hours. Stir occasionally to prevent sticking and add more water if necessary.

YIELD: *6–8 servings*

Chili Pie

Chili Pie is chili in a casserole form. It is a perfect way to use any leftover chili, and the melted cheese and crunchy chips make it a different and tasty way to serve this favorite.

A variation from the casserole version and a real Texas treat is Chili Pie "in the bag." The small individual bags of corn chips are used. Before the bags are opened, the chips are crushed. The bag is then opened and the hot chili is spooned into the chip bag. The onions and cheese are added and the Chili Pie is eaten out of the bag. Not only tasty—but fun as well!

2½ cups crushed corn chips or tostados	1 cup grated Longhorn or Cheddar cheese
1 onion, chopped	2 cups chili, heated

Place 1½ cups crushed chips in a 1½-quart casserole or baking dish and sprinkle with chopped onion and ½ cup grated cheese. Pour heated chili over cheese and top with remaining chips and grated cheese.

Bake at 350° for 15–20 minutes, until it is heated through and cheese is melted. YIELD: *4 servings*

Lone Star Chili

6 dried red peppers	3 cloves garlic, minced
8 cups water	2 onions, chopped
2 pounds beef, cut into 1-inch cubes	2 tablespoons vegetable oil
	salt to taste

Wash peppers and remove stems and seeds. In a large pan, cover peppers with 8 cups water and bring to a boil. Lower heat to medium, cover, and simmer for 20–30 minutes. Remove peppers from pan and reserve the liquid.

Gently peel the skin from the peppers. If skin is difficult to remove, scrape the pulp off carefully with a spoon. Combine the pulp from all 6 peppers with 1 cup of reserved liquid in a blender and mix until smooth.

Sauté beef, garlic, and onions in oil until beef is browned. Add the pepper mixture and stir in remaining liquid from peppers. Cook over very low heat for 3–4 hours or until meat is tender and the liquid has reduced by half and is thickened. Add salt to taste. YIELD: *6–8 servings*

Chili and Beans

1 pound ground beef	6 ounces tomato sauce
1 clove garlic, minced	¾ cup water
2–4 tablespoons chili powder	salt to taste
2 teaspoons flour	1 cup cooked pinto beans
1 teaspoon ground cumin (comino)	

In a large skillet, brown ground beef and garlic. Drain off any excess grease. Combine chili powder, flour, and cumin and sprinkle over beef. Stir lightly to distribute. Add tomato sauce to water and pour over meat, stirring as it is added. Season with salt and simmer 10–15 minutes. Add cooked beans and continue cooking until beans are heated through.   YIELD: *4 servings*

Carne con Chiles

The translation of this dish is "meat with chilies," but don't send for the fire trucks yet. Experiment with the pepper until it is right for you. It can be anything from mild to "three alarm."

The meat is very tender and the sauce a rich color with a savory taste. Serve it with Sopa de Fideo (Chapter 6), Guacamole (Chapter 3), and flour tortillas for a great meal, or just fold some into a flour tortilla as a Burrito.

3 pounds lean stew meat	2 cloves garlic
3 tablespoons oil	1 teaspoon cumin (comino)
5 tomatoes	salt to taste
2 or 3 fresh or canned jalapeño peppers	

Brown stew meat in oil in a large pan over high heat. Set whole, unpeeled tomatoes and jalapeños on top of meat, cover, and steam for 10–15 minutes. Remove tomatoes and jalapeños and peel. Place in a blender along with garlic and process until smooth. Add this sauce to beef, along with the cumin and salt. Cover and cook slowly for 1½–2 hours.   YIELD: *4–6 servings*

Corn Dogs

Corn Dogs are a meal on a stick, and they are always a big hit at home as well as at country fairs, carnivals, and rodeos. They are easy to prepare and fun to eat for children of all ages.

They may be prepared ahead and frozen. To reheat, bake at 400° for 10–15 minutes (do not thaw before heating).

1½ cups flour	1⅓ cups milk
1 tablespoon sugar	1 tablespoon oil
½ teaspoon salt	2 tablespoons prepared mustard
1½ teaspoons baking powder	10 frankfurters
¾ cup cornmeal	½ cup flour
1 egg	oil for frying

Sift together 1½ cups flour, sugar, salt, and baking powder. Stir in cornmeal. Combine egg, milk, 1 tablespoon oil, and mustard and add to dry ingredients, mixing until smooth.

Wipe frankfurters dry and roll in ½ cup flour. Dip into batter and coat and deep fry in hot oil (375°) until golden brown. Drain on paper towels. Serve as is or insert a wooden skewer in the end of each one.   YIELD: *10*

Boiled Tongue

Our father began working in a butcher shop in New Braunfels at the age of seven. He was taught, and so we learned, that when you butchered a cow nothing should go to waste. Our grandmother taught us to keep an open mind. Fortunately we learned both of these lessons, or we might never have tried Boiled Tongue. We also would have missed out on a real taste treat. The tongue is sliced wafer-thin and used for sandwiches with homemade bread, mayonnaise, and crisp dill pickles, or it can be used in casseroles or for Pickled Tongue in Mayonnaise (Chapter 1).

1 fresh beef tongue (2½–3 pounds)	1 teaspoon peppercorns
	2 bay leaves
1 teaspoon vinegar	1 onion, sliced

Place tongue in large pan and cover with water. Add remaining ingredients and bring to a boil. Cover and simmer 2½–3 hours or until tender. Remove cover and allow to cool in stock.

When cool, remove skin from tongue and refrigerate to chill. YIELD: *2½–3 pounds*

Ham Steaks and Red-Eye Gravy

Ham Steaks, Biscuits (Chapter 8), and Red-Eye Gravy are a trio from the past and one that cannot be beat. Some people simply add water to the pan drippings to make this gravy. But the chuck-wagon boss would say that it is the coffee that guarantees it is real Red-Eye Gravy, and who would argue?

2 tablespoons vegetable oil	½ cup water
2 pounds uncooked ham steaks, about ¼ inch thick	2 tablespoons brewed coffee

In a large skillet, heat oil and sauté steaks over medium high heat, one at a time, until brown. When all steaks are browned, return to skillet, add the water, and cover. Lower heat and simmer for 15–20 minutes or until steaks are thoroughly done. Remove steaks to a heated platter and keep warm.

Measure the pan drippings and add enough water to make 1 cup of liquid. Return to pan and heat, scraping bottoms and sides of pan to loosen any brown pieces. Stir in coffee. Serve gravy over the steaks.   YIELD: *4 servings*

Pioneer Pork Pie

One hundred years ago this Pork Pie was probably cooked in a big cast iron Dutch oven hung over an open fire. Fortunately, we do not have to go through all that these days to enjoy the same savory dishes.

This pie is also evidence that leftovers do not have to be dull or boring; it is a colorful, hearty dish that is great "back to basics" fare.

4 small carrots, sliced
4 small potatoes, cubed
1 medium onion, cut into eighths
1 cup fresh or frozen peas
4 tablespoons pork drippings or
   oil

3 tablespoons flour
2½ cups liquids—pan drippings
   and water
2 cups cubed cooked pork
Pioneer Pastry for topping (see
   below)

Place carrots, potatoes, onion, and peas (if fresh) in a saucepan and cover with water. (If using frozen peas, add them the last 5 minutes of cooking.) Cover and cook until tender—about 20 minutes. Drain.

In a skillet, combine pork drippings or oil with flour over medium heat. Blend until smooth and beginning to brown. Gradually add 2½ cups liquid and stir until thickened. Stir in cubed pork and cooked vegetables and pour into a greased 1½-quart casserole.

Top with pastry and bake at 425° for 10–12 minutes or until crust is golden brown.   YIELD: *6 servings*

PIONEER PASTRY

1 cup flour
1 teaspoon baking powder
¼ teaspoon salt

½ teaspoon sugar
¼ cup shortening
¼ cup milk

Sift dry ingredients together and cut in shortening. Stir in milk to make a soft dough. Turn out on floured board and knead until smooth. Roll dough to ¼-inch thickness. Cut into 1-inch-wide strips and crisscross over top of casserole, crimping along sides. Alternatively, dough may be cut into a circle to cover the entire casserole. Crimp around edges and make 10–12 slits in the top. Brush the crust with melted butter, if desired.

Chorizo

Chorizo (cho-REE-zo) is a savory beef and pork sausage with just a hint of chili powder. It is used in a variety of Mexican dishes and makes a good breakfast sausage. (See recipe for Huevos con Chorizo in Chapter 5.)

1 large onion, finely chopped
1 pound ground beef
½ pound ground pork butt
2 teaspoons chili powder
2 teaspoons oregano

½ teaspoon cumin (comino)
¼ teaspoon cinnamon
1 teaspoon salt
5 tablespoons vinegar

Combine all ingredients.
Use as bulk sausage, put into casings, or form into patties. Refrigerate or freeze.   YIELD: *2½ pounds*

Pan-Fried Pork Chops

Pan-Fried Pork Chops are definitely a finger food, as you will want to get every last morsel off the bones.

Be sure to make Cream Gravy (Chapter 7), using the pan drippings and any of the remaining flour mixture. Round off the meal with rice, a fresh green vegetable, and some warm applesauce or stewed fruit.

oil for frying
1 cup flour
1 teaspoon salt

½ teaspoon pepper
12 pork chops, ¼–½ inch thick

Heat ¼ inch oil in a heavy skillet. Combine flour, salt, and pepper and dredge pork chops until well coated.

Fry in hot oil until golden brown.   YIELD: *4–6 servings*

Stuffed Pork Chops

This recipe turns pork chops into real party fare. For convenience, they can be prepared ahead through the first hour of baking and then refrigerated. When ready to serve, brush them with the glaze and bake at 375° until they are glazed and heated through—about 20–30 minutes.

8 large pork chops, 1¼–1½ inches
   thick
½ pound seasoned pork sausage
⅔ cup chopped onion
⅔ cup chopped celery
1 large apple, finely chopped
5 slices dry, toasted bread
1–1¼ cups water
¼ cup chopped pecans
1 egg, beaten
¼–½ cup water
4 tablespoons currant or other
   tart jelly

With a sharp paring knife, cut a large pocket in each pork chop, not more than 2 inches wide. Set aside.

In a heavy skillet, sauté sausage (breaking into small pieces), onion, celery, and apple over medium heat until sausage has browned. Allow to cool.

In a mixing bowl, break up dry bread and moisten with 1 cup water. Add pecans, beaten egg, and sausage mixture to bread. Mix well, adding remaining ¼ cup water, if needed, to make a moist dressing. Adjust seasonings as needed.

Firmly pack the pocket of each pork chop with dressing mixture. Close pockets with small skewers or toothpicks.

Arrange pork chops in a large baking dish and add ¼–½ cup water. Bake at 325° for 1 hour.

Fifteen to twenty minutes before serving, dissolve jelly in a small saucepan over low heat. Brush jelly over pork chops and return to oven, baking at 375° for 10–15 minutes or until chops are evenly browned and glazed. Remove from oven, remove skewers, and serve immediately.   YIELD: *8 servings*

Spareribs and Sauerkraut

Sauerkraut is a German classic, and when it is combined with spareribs the result is fantastic. The sauerkraut absorbs some of the meat's flavor, which serves to enhance its own. The apples and new potatoes turn this into a one-dish meal. Have finger bowls or plenty of napkins on hand, though, because these ribs, like Pan-Fried Pork Chops, really aren't suitable for eating with a fork.

Pork chops can be substituted for the spareribs if desired. Simply brown them in a little oil before assembling the casserole.

4 pounds spareribs
5–6 cups sauerkraut
8 small new potatoes, halved
  (optional)

1 apple, diced (optional)
1 onion, chopped
4 tablespoons brown sugar
2 cups water

Cut spareribs into serving-size pieces, 3–4 ribs each.

Spread 2 cups sauerkraut in the bottom of a 3–4-quart casserole. Top with half the ribs, half the potato pieces, half the diced apple, and half the onion. Add another layer of 2 cups sauerkraut and repeat with remaining ribs, potatoes, apple, and onion. Top with remaining sauerkraut.

Combine brown sugar and water and pour over casserole. Cover and bake at 325° for 2–3 hours.   YIELD: *4–6 servings*

Scrapple

Scrapple is a cornmeal-sausage mixture from the days of the frontier. After it is set, it is pan-fried to a golden, crispy brown. Make it a part of a hearty breakfast, serving it with molasses and fried eggs on top or on the side.

1 pound bulk pork sausage
2 cups yellow cornmeal
6 cups water
1 teaspoon salt

½ teaspoon garlic powder
½–1 teaspoon cayenne pepper
oil for frying

Place the sausage in a large saucepan, with water to cover. Bring to a boil, cover, and simmer 30–40 minutes. Pour sausage into a colander to drain.

Place cornmeal in the saucepan, add 2 cups water, and mix until smooth. Add the drained sausage and the remaining 4 cups water. Add seasonings, cover, and cook over low heat until thick (20–30 minutes).

Pour into a greased loaf pan and allow to cool. Cover and refrigerate overnight.

To serve, slice scrapple ¼ inch thick. Fry in a small amount of oil until browned and crisp around the edges.

YIELD: *1 9-by-5-by-3-inch loaf pan*

Venison Backstrap

The backstrap is the tenderloin or fillet of the deer, and, as with beef, it is considered the choicest of the cuts. It can be used in many ways, but no one would dare "waste" it by grinding it for chili and the like, since the lesser cuts work just as well for these.

One favorite preparation which utilizes the full potential of the backstrap is a mock filet mignon. The bacon not only enhances the flavor of the venison but also adds a necessary amount of fat, which is needed because the meat itself is naturally very lean; precautions should be taken to keep the meat from becoming too dry.

Soaking the venison or any wild game or game birds in buttermilk reduces the "wild" or "gamey" taste. To soak or not to soak is a matter of personal pereference. Some of the older generation may welcome the "gamey" taste as a flavor of the bygone days when meat was not so overly processed.

1 2½–3-pound venison backstrap　　**6 bacon slices**
2 cups buttermilk　　**salt and garlic powder to taste**

Slice venison backstrap across the grain into 1½-inch filets. Place in a bowl and cover with buttermilk. Let soak overnight in the refrigerator.

Remove from buttermilk and rinse. Dry each filet, season with salt and garlic powder to taste and wrap with a bacon slice around the edge, securing ends with a toothpick.

Grill over high heat, 4–6 inches from heat, for 6–8 minutes for medium doneness.   YIELD: *6 servings*

Venison/Pork Sausage

When the triumphant hunters return with their prize of a deer, each family member eyes his or her favorite part with mouth-watering visions of backstrap steaks, barbecued roasts, fried steaks, chili stew, or venison sausage. As the deer is being butchered, everyone is there to put in an order for a special cut. The remaining venison is ground and used for the sausage, which is really the best part of all.

Regardless of the work involved, we all have fond memories of "helping" our grandfather make these delicious rings. Even those with a squeamish stomach pitched in with visions of the finished product in mind. The meat was ground, the seasoning added, and the meat ground again. The mixture was kneaded until our shoulders ached and the sausage began to get firm. Meanwhile, the casings were cleaned and soaked and then cut into strips. The string was measured and cut, and we were ready to stuff. Each link was stuffed with care, allowing no air bubbles inside and making sure the casings didn't split. After the links were tied, they were hung in the smokehouse on long sticks to "drip" for 24 hours. The next day the fire was built for the smoking process to begin.

With great anticipation we tended the fire and waited for the day the sausage was ready. After the smoking was completed, the sausage was hung for a few days to continue drying. It was at this point that everyone had a different idea of when the sausage was ready. Some preferred it softer, so it could be steamed and eaten. Others, with more patience, waited until it was hard enough to break apart and eat right off the ring. This was the kind that you could put into your saddlebags or back pockets and take off with.

Some of the sausage was not put into casings, but saved for pan sausage. This would be fried in patties or crumbled and mixed with scrambled eggs or added to beans.

However it was eaten, it was wonderful, and so much so that we continue to make the sausage whenever we get the chance. We still use Grandpa Adolph's hand-cranked stuffer and his smokehouse, reminiscing the whole time about those bygone days. Modern conveniences would no doubt make the job much easier, but the experience would never be the same.

If you don't have access to a smokehouse or a place to dry the sausage, it can be frozen immediately after stuffing or forming and kept for several months.

Also, boneless beef can be substituted for the venison, if desired or if venison is not available. The proportions should be changed to 60 percent beef–40 percent pork if beef is used, and the seasonings remain the same.

12½ pounds boneless venison
12½ pounds pork butt, boned
⅔ cup salt
5–6 cloves garlic, minced
1½ tablespoons black pepper

1½ tablespoons cayenne pepper
5 pounds casings for sausage, thoroughly washed in warm water and left to soak in clear water until ready to use

Grind all meat together through coarse blade.

Rub salt into minced garlic until the mixture is of the consistency of coarse cornmeal. Add garlic mixture, black pepper, and cayenne pepper to ground meat and mix thoroughly.

Grind meat a second time through fine blade. Mix and knead the meat until the sausage mixture can be formed into large, firm balls.

Stuff sausage into casings, making certain no air remains in the casing. Cut filled casings into 12-inch sections. Bring both open ends of each section together, forming a ring. Using a good string, tie ends closed and then tie ends together.

As an alternative, form sausage into serving-size patties—about ⅓–½ pound each.

To serve sausage rings, place 1 or 2 rings in a large skillet filled with 1 inch of water. Cover and steam over low to medium heat for 35–45 minutes. To avoid loss of juices, do not pierce casing while cooking.

Patties are best pan fried in a heavy skillet over medium heat until browned. Allow approximately ½ pound per serving.

YIELD: *25 pounds*

5. Poultry, Seafood, and Eggs

Chicken and Dumplings

"Chicken 'n Dumplings" is a meal out of the past, reminiscent of a big Sunday lunch at Grandma's. If you have never tried it, you do not know what you are missing. The light dumpling sauce and tender chicken make a wonderful combination. If you have not tried it for years, try it again soon. You will enjoy a taste you have missed.

4 tablespoons vegetable oil
½ cup flour
salt and pepper to taste
4–5 pounds chicken, cut into
    pieces
5 cups hot water
1 large onion, quartered
2 stalks celery, coarsely chopped
1 carrot, sliced

1 teaspoon salt
1½ cups flour
2 teaspoons baking powder
½ teaspoon salt
1 teaspoon chopped parsley
3 tablespoons shortening
¾ cup milk
½ cup milk
5 tablespoons flour

Heat oil in a Dutch oven or large pot. Combine ½ cup flour with salt and pepper to taste and dust each chicken piece. Brown the chicken lightly in hot oil. Drain off remaining oil and add 4 cups of hot water, onion, celery, carrot, and 1 tablespoon salt. Simmer covered, for 45–60 minutes or until chicken is tender. Remove chicken; strain, reserving stock. Bone chicken if desired.

For dumplings, sift 1½ cups flour, 2 teaspoons baking powder, and ½ teaspoon salt together and add the chopped parsley. Toss to distribute. Cut in shortening and slowly add ¾ cup milk to form a soft dough. Set aside.

In a small bowl, slowly add ½ cup milk to 5 tablespoons flour. Add a small amount of chicken stock to the flour mixture, mixing until smooth. Bring remainder of reserved chicken stock to a boil, lower heat until stock is just simmering, and gradually add milk and flour mixture. Stir until thickened and return to a boil. Add chicken pieces and drop dumpling dough by heaping tablespoons into boiling broth. Simmer uncovered for 10 minutes. Cover and simmer an additional 10 minutes.

Serve chicken with dumplings and gravy spooned over both.

YIELD: *4–6 servings*

Texas Fried Chicken

Tender, succulent chicken inside and a crisp, golden batter . . . what more can be said about this "all-American" favorite? But, do yourself a favor: make it yourself just once. There is no comparing it to the "fast-food" variety.

18 pieces chicken
2 cups buttermilk
shortening for frying (oil may be substituted)
2 cups flour
2 teaspoons salt
1 teaspoon pepper

Place chicken pieces in a large bowl and cover with buttermilk. Let stand for 30–60 minutes.

Melt shortening in a large heavy skillet, ½ inch deep. Combine flour, salt, and pepper. Dip chicken in flour mixture to coat. Over medium high heat, heat shortening to 375°. Fry 4 or 5 pieces at a time. If chicken browns too quickly, lower heat slightly. Cook until golden brown and tender. The dark meat pieces should take 15–20 minutes, the white meat, 10–15 minutes.

Drain chicken on paper towels and serve hot or cold.

YIELD: *6 servings*

Stewed Chicken

The chicken in this dish is first browned and then stewed until it is "fall-off-the-bone" tender. The remaining pan juices make an extra special gravy to serve over egg noodles, rice, or mashed potatoes. This is a good dish to make with less tender chickens (broilers or hens).

3–4 pounds chicken, cut into pieces
6–8 tablespoons flour
2 teaspoons paprika
1 teaspoon salt
1 teaspoon black pepper
4 tablespoons butter or rendered chicken fat
2 cups water

Coat chicken pieces liberally with a mixture of the flour, paprika, salt, and pepper. (Reserve any remaining flour mixture.) Brown chicken thoroughly in butter or chicken fat in a heavy Dutch oven over medium heat.

When all chicken is browned, add 1½ cups water and simmer, covered, over low heat for 40–50 minutes or until tender.

Remove chicken to serving dish and keep warm. Combine the remaining ½ cup water with 2 tablespoons of the reserved flour mixture and mix until smooth. Bring juices in pan to a simmer and gradually add flour-water mixture, stirring constantly until thickened.

Pour gravy over chicken.   YIELD: *4–6 servings*

Barbecued Chicken Texas Style

A Lone Star classic. Follow the directions here and under Texas Style Barbecue (Chapter 4), and the result will be chicken with a crisp, golden skin and tender, juicy meat.

4 2½-pound fryers, split or quartered
seasonings to taste
Basting Sauce for Barbecue (Chapter 7)

Trim any excess fat, wing tips, tail, and excess skin from chicken. Rinse well and pat dry. Season as desired.

Grill 8 inches above coals, with grill covered, cooking slowly for 1½–2 hours, or until chicken is evenly browned and tender. Turn and baste with sauce every 20–30 minutes.   YIELD: *8 servings*

Chicken Chalupas

Refried beans, chicken, and guacamole make a winning combination for chalupas.

oil for frying
12 corn tortillas
2 cups Refried Beans (Chapter 6)

3 cups cooked chicken, shredded
shredded lettuce
2 cups Guacamole (Chapter 3)

In a small frying pan, heat ½ inch oil over high heat. Fry tortillas, one at a time, until crisp. Drain on a paper towel.

Heat refried beans in a small saucepan.

To assemble chalupas, spread a portion of beans on each fried tortilla and top with a layer of shredded chicken, a layer of shredded lettuce, and a spoonful of guacamole.   YIELD: *6 servings*

Chicken Taco Filling

This chicken dish is a delicious filling for the traditional Taco (see Chapter 4), or try it in a soft taco. Prepare the shells for soft tacos by immersing corn tortillas in ½ inch hot oil only until they are soft. Drain on paper towels. Spoon filling down the center of each tortilla and fold in half or roll. Serve immediately with grated Monterrey Jack cheese, lettuce, and Guacamole (Chapter 3).

3 tablespoons oil
1 medium onion, chopped
1 large clove garlic, minced
2 cups cooked chicken

1½ cups canned tomatoes and
  green chilies with juice
½ teaspoon cumin (comino)
salt and pepper to taste

In a heavy skillet, heat oil and sauté onion, garlic, and chicken, using two forks to stir and shred chicken. Cook over medium heat until chicken starts to brown and gets crisp around the edges.

Add tomatoes and green chilies with juice, breaking the tomatoes into small pieces as you add them. Add cumin, salt, and pepper.

Continue cooking over medium heat until all liquid has cooked down—about 10 minutes. Scrape bottom of pan frequently to prevent sticking.   YIELD: *8–10 servings*

Cowboy Chicken Casserole

The ingredients in this layered casserole combine for a Tex-Mex fiesta in one dish. A lasting Texas favorite, it can be prepared ahead and frozen, before baking, for 2–3 months.

2 2½-pound chickens
4 tablespoons butter
4 tablespoons flour
1 cup milk
½ teaspoon salt
½ teaspoon garlic powder
1½ cups canned tomatoes,
  chopped

½ cup canned green chilies,
  chopped
1 onion, chopped
12 corn tortillas
2 cups grated Longhorn or
  Cheddar cheese

Cover chickens with water in a large pot and simmer 45–60 minutes or until tender. Allow to cool, then remove skin and bone. Reserve stock.

In a saucepan, over low heat, melt butter, add flour, and blend until smooth. Combine 1 cup of the reserved stock with milk and gradually add to flour mixture, stirring constantly until thickened, to make a cream sauce. Remove from heat and season with salt and garlic powder. Stir in tomatoes, chilies, and onion and set aside.

Bring remaining chicken stock to a boil. Dip each tortilla in stock to soften. Cut tortillas into 2-inch strips.

To assemble casserole, cover the bottom of a 9-by-13-inch casserole with one-third of the tortilla strips. Layer half of the boned chicken over tortillas and top with half of the creamed tomato mixture. Sprinkle 1 cup grated cheese over sauce. Add another layer of tortillas, top with remaining chicken, spoon over remaining cream sauce, and top with remaining tortillas. Sprinkle remaining cheese over top.

Bake at 350° for 30–40 minutes or until sauce is bubbly and cheese has melted.   YIELD: *8 servings*

Quail and Dove

Quail and dove are abundant in Texas, and hunting these game birds is a favorite sport. Because they are so plentiful, Texans have devised many ways to prepare them.

Barbecued Quail with Bacon can be prepared right over the fire at the campsite. Doves Stuffed with Sausage, when served with wild rice, make an elegant dinner party dish, and Doves in Beer is a complete one-dish meal.

Some of the best hunting is close to the Mexican border. Many of the restaurants in the small borders towns specialize in preparing these delicious game birds. Thus, many of the recipes have a Mexican flair, as in Mexican Fried Quail.

Barbecued Quail with Bacon

8 whole quail	4 tablespoons butter
2–4 cups milk	4 slices bacon
1 apple, finely chopped	

Soak the quail, in enough milk to cover, overnight.

Fill each cavity with 2 tablespoons chopped apple and ½ tablespoon butter. Wrap each with half a slice of bacon and secure with a toothpick.

Grill over a medium charcoal fire, 4–6 inches from heat, until bacon is done and birds are browned and tender, about 20 minutes.   YIELD: *4 servings*

Mexican Fried Quail

8 quail, whole or split
2–4 cups milk
oil for frying
1 cup flour

½ teaspoon salt
¼ teaspoon pepper
2–3 tablespoons chili powder
1–1½ cups water or milk

Soak quail, in enough milk to cover, overnight.

In a heavy skillet, heat ½ inch oil to 350°. Combine flour, salt, pepper, and chili powder. Dip soaked quail in flour mixture and fry 10–15 minutes, until browned and tender. Set aside.

Pour off all but 2 tablespoons oil in skillet. Add 2 tablespoons of the remaining flour mixture and blend well, scraping sides and bottom of skillet. Slowly stir in 1–1½ cups water or milk and cook slowly until gravy is of desired consistency. Adjust seasonings.

YIELD: *4 servings*

Doves in Beer

8 whole doves
salt and pepper to taste
¼ cup oil
1 onion, finely chopped

1 cup sliced mushrooms
1 clove garlic, minced
2 cups uncooked rice
2 12-ounce cans beer

Rub doves with salt and pepper and brown in hot oil in a Dutch oven over high heat. When lightly browned, remove from pan and set aside. In remaining oil, sauté onions, mushrooms, garlic, and rice over medium high heat 3–5 minutes, until rice begins to brown. Add doves and beer; cover and simmer for 45–60 minutes or until doves are tender and rice is done.

YIELD: *4–6 servings*

Doves Stuffed with Sausage

½ pound pork sausage
⅔ cup chopped onion
⅔ cup chopped celery
1 clove garlic, minced
5 slices dry bread, crumbled
1 cup chicken stock

1 egg, beaten
16 whole doves
salt and pepper to taste
1 cup vegetable oil
2 cups chicken stock

Combine sausage, onion, celery, and garlic and cook over medium heat until sausage is browned and crumbly. Drain off any grease.

In a small bowl, combine crumbled bread, 1 cup chicken stock, and beaten egg. Add to sausage mixture and blend well.

Loosely stuff each dove with sausage-bread mixture. Season doves with salt and pepper, as desired.

Brown 3 or 4 stuffed doves at a time in 1 cup oil in a heavy skillet over high heat for 3–5 minutes. When all are browned, place in a large oven-proof casserole and add 2 cups chicken stock. Cover and bake at 350° for 40–60 minutes until doves are tender. Remove cover and bake an additional 15 minutes to brown birds.

YIELD: *8 servings*

Grilled Shrimp

The marinade in the recipe imparts a tangy taste of lemon with a hint of garlic. Grilling over coals enhances these flavors.

1½ pounds large uncooked shrimp (about 1 ounce each)	2 cloves garlic, pressed
1 cup vegetable oil	2 bay leaves
juice of 3–4 lemons	½ teaspoon salt

Peel shrimp, leaving tails on. Butterfly the shrimp by splitting each one open, making a cut along the top that goes all the way to the bottom but not through the bottom. Place in a glass bowl.

Combine remaining ingredients and pour over shrimp. Marinate 2–4 hours in the refrigerator, stirring occasionally.

Grill over very hot coals, 4–6 inches from heat, for 3–4 minutes per side, depending on size of shrimp. Baste with remaining marinade when done.   YIELD: *4 servings*

Butterfly Fried Shrimp

Almost everyone loves fried shrimp, and Texans are no exception. When the big jumbo shrimp come in, we usually "butterfly" them. When they are split and opened like this, they not only look prettier on the plate, but also cook faster and are more tender.

The beer batter for the fried shrimp is light and crisp and goes especially well with Cocktail Sauce (Chapter 7).

2 pounds uncooked shrimp (about 1 ounce each)	1 tablespoon vegetable oil
1 cup flour	1 cup beer
1 teaspoon baking powder	½ cup flour
1 teaspoon salt	oil for frying

Peel shrimp, leaving the tails on. To butterfly shrimp, make a cut starting along the top of each shrimp and going all the way to the bottom but not through the bottom.

Make batter by combining 1 cup flour, baking powder, salt, 1 tablespoon oil, and beer. Mix with a fork or wire whisk until smooth. Set aside and allow to rest for 20–30 minutes.

To fry shrimp, heat 3 inches of oil in a large saucepan to 375°. With shrimp spread open, dip in ½ cup flour and then into batter. Drop into hot oil and fry 3–4 minutes or until golden brown. Drain on paper towels. Serve immediately.   YIELD: *6–8 servings*

Pickled Shrimp

This recipe is a delightfully easy way to prepare shrimp and is delicious as an appetizer as well as a main dish.

1–1½ pounds cooked, peeled
   shrimp
1 onion, thinly sliced
1 lemon, thinly sliced
4 bay leaves
½ cup capers

⅔ cup vegetable oil
⅔ cup white vinegar
6 tablespoons lemon juice
1½ teaspoons salt
dash Tabasco sauce

In a large glass jar or bowl, layer shrimp alternately with onion slices, lemon slices, bay leaves, and capers.

Combine remaining ingredients and pour over the shrimp. Cover and refrigerate for at least 24 hours and up to 3 days.
                    YIELD: *1–1½ pounds*

Shrimp Boiled in Beer

When you ask Texans what they are going to do during the summer months, nine times out of ten they will tell you that they are going to "the coast." "The coast," or the beach as most people know it, is a string of narrow islands situated in the Gulf of Mexico which follow the contour of the mainland. Rich in wildlife, some of the areas have been designated as National Wildlife Refuges. The longest of the islands is Padre Island, which is a National Seashore and a favorite vacation spot.

A trip to the coast means sandy beaches, rolling sand dunes, crystal clear water, and fresh Gulf shrimp. If you're lucky, you can buy them right off the shrimp boats; otherwise, they are available at the local markets.

An easy and delicious way to enjoy them is to serve them boiled. Cover the table with newspaper and place a big bowl of cold, boiled shrimp in the center. Add a bowl of Cocktail Sauce (Chapter 7) and a pile of napkins and ring the dinner bell. The diners peel and eat the shrimp, leaving the shells on the paper. Afterward, remove the bowls, wrap the paper up (shells and all), and you're through.

2 pounds raw shrimp	**2 bay leaves**
2 12-ounce cans beer (or enough to cover)	**1 small onion, sliced**
	1 tablespoon peppercorns
1 lemon, thinly sliced	**2 cloves garlic, chopped**

Combine all ingredients in a large pot and bring to a boil. Cook 3–5 minutes or until shrimp begin to turn pink and are tender. Drain and chill before serving.   YIELD: *2–4 servings*

Fried Catfish

Some Texans say that there is only one fish to fry, and that is a catfish. One reason may be because they are as much fun to catch as they are to eat.

Catfish stories thrive around the rivers and lakes of Texas. There are the elusive granddaddies that live in the still, deep waters of the Pedernales River or the "one that got away" in Lake LBJ.

The methods of catching the fish are as numerous and innovative as the stories. Cane poles can be used with the fisherman's own secret bloodbait, a special concoction that has been allowed to ferment in cheesecloth. If you are not too energetic you can use throw lines. The lines are hung from tree limbs all along the bank, with a bell attached to each line. The angler sits back and enjoys a nap until awakened by the bell signaling a catch.

Whether you catch them yourself or buy them in a market, you are sure to enjoy them pan-fried.

2 pounds catfish filets	**oil for frying**
1½–2 cups cornmeal	**1 lemon**
1 teaspoon salt	

Dredge each filet, to coat, in cornmeal seasoned with salt.

Heat ½ inch oil in a frying pan over high heat to 350–375°. Fry filets, turning occasionally, until golden brown (3–4 minutes). Just before removing from pan, squeeze a small amount of lemon juice on each filet. Remove and drain on paper towels.

YIELD: *4–6 servings*

Huevos Rancheros

The aroma of fresh corn tortillas and a delicate tomato sauce coming from the ranch kitchen was all that was needed to bring everyone running to breakfast for Huevos Rancheros (ranch style eggs). All the cook needed to know was whether the eggs should be poached, scrambled, or fried, and this traditional Tex-Mex breakfast was on its way. The eggs could also be poached in the ranchero sauce itself: make four indentations in the sauce, drop in the eggs, cover, and cook 3–5 minutes.

However, you do not need a ranch and a cook to bring people running to the table. The results are guaranteed wherever or whenever Huevos Rancheros are served, whether for breakfast, brunch, or late night supper.

1 tablespoon bacon drippings or oil	**½ teaspoon salt**
	oil for frying
1 small onion, chopped	**4 corn tortillas**
2 cups canned tomatoes, chopped, with juice	**4 eggs**
	1 cup grated Cheddar or Monterrey Jack cheese (optional)
½ cup canned green chilies, chopped, with liquid	

In a large skillet over medium heat, heat bacon drippings or oil and sauté onion until transparent. Add tomatoes and green chilies, with their juices, and season with salt. Cook over medium high heat about 10 minutes, until almost all the liquid is reduced.

Heat ½ inch oil in a small skillet over high heat. Dip each tortilla in oil to soften (1–2 seconds).

Scramble, fry, or poach the eggs.

To assemble, top each tortilla with an egg. Spoon the ranchero sauce over the egg. If desired, sprinkle grated cheese over the sauce and run under the broiler to melt.　　YIELD: *4 servings*

Huevos con Chorizo

As versatile as they are delicious, Huevos con Chorizo are ideal for Sunday morning breakfast, brunch for a crowd, a midnight supper, breakfast around the campfire, or a lunchbox treat. The sausage and eggs are cooked in one pan, so they are quick and easy as well. Serve them with warm Flour Tortillas (Chapter 8), Hot Sauce (Chapter 7), Refried Beans (Chapter 6), and fresh fruit for a brunch or supper. For more casual fare, spoon the eggs directly on a tortilla and fold it in half for a breakfast taco; or, wrap the folded tortilla in foil and pop it in a lunchbox.

1½ pounds Chorizo (Chapter 4)　　**salt and pepper to taste**
12–14 eggs, well beaten

In a heavy skillet, cook the chorizo over medium heat, breaking it up as it cooks, until browned. Pour out on paper towels to drain.

Add seasonings to beaten eggs and stir in chorizo. Pour into the heavy skillet and cook over medium heat until eggs are firm and set.   YIELD: *12 servings*

Chilaquiles

Chilaquiles are a unique version of scrambled eggs. They should be served with Picante Sauce (Chapter 7).

3–4 tablespoons lard or vegetable
 oil
6 stale corn tortillas, broken or
 cut into ⅜-inch strips
6 eggs, beaten
½ cup chopped onion

½ cup canned green chilies,
 chopped
½ teaspoon salt
1 cup shredded Longhorn or
 Cheddar cheese

Heat oil over high heat in a large frying pan. When oil is hot, fry tortillas until crisp (1–2 minutes). Drain on paper towels.

Combine eggs, onion, chilies, and salt. Return fried tortillas to pan and pour in egg mixture. Cook until almost set, add cheese, and continue cooking until cheese melts and eggs are firm.
                                                    YIELD: *4 servings*

Breakfast Casserole

This recipe is perfect for the impromptu, carefree type of entertaining Texans do so well. Since it is prepared the day before, you can enjoy an elegant brunch right along with your guests. With bread, sausage, eggs, and milk, it is a one-dish meal. All that is needed to round out your menu is a fruit plate and a pot of steaming coffee. For Christmas morning or New Year's Day, turn it into a champagne brunch just by popping a cork.

1½ pounds pork sausage
½ cup chopped onion
½ cup chopped bell pepper
1 clove garlic, minced
½ cup sliced mushrooms
6 slices cubed bread (crusts
   removed)

1 cup grated Cheddar cheese
2 cups scalded milk
3 beaten eggs
1 teaspoon baking power
salt and pepper to taste

Sauté sausage, onions, pepper, garlic, and mushrooms in a large skillet over medium heat for 3–5 minutes, until sausage is done.

In a 9-by-13-inch casserole, layer sausage mixture alternately with bread cubes and grated cheese.

Combine milk, eggs, baking powder, salt, and pepper and beat with a wire whisk until smooth. Pour over casserole and cover.

Refrigerate overnight.

To serve, bake uncovered, at 350° for 1 hour.   YIELD: *8 servings*

Deviled Eggs

Deviled Eggs are a picnic standard or the perfect touch for a luncheon relish tray. Experiment with the filling: try dill pickles instead of the sweet, capers, pimiento, or whatever tickles your fancy. For a dressier egg use a pastry tube for the filling.

6 hard-boiled eggs
¼ cup mayonnaise
1 tablespoon prepared mustard
¼ teaspoon salt
dash of pepper

1 teaspoon minced celery
1 teaspoon minced onion
1 tablespoon sweet pickle relish
paprika and parsley (optional)

Peel eggs and slice in half lengthwise. Carefully remove the yolks and place in a shallow bowl. Using a fork, mash yolks until you have fine crumbs. Add mayonnaise, mustard, salt, pepper, celery, onion, and pickle relish and blend well.

Fill the hollows of the egg whites with the yolk mixture. Sprinkle with paprika and garnish with parsley, if desired. Chill before serving.   YIELD: *1 dozen*

Pickled Eggs

Before Texas was crisscrossed with the massive interstate high-ways, small highways and "farm-to-market" roads wound their way across our state and connected our cities and towns. When traveling during our childhood, our family would stop for gas in such towns as Comfort, Lone Oak, Skidmore, and Beeville. The gas station (which we called a "filling station") would most likely be combined with a general store or café. On the counter by the cash register would be gallon jars of pickled eggs, dill pickles, and/or jerky. We would choose our treat, and then be on our way. The days of those stops are mostly gone now, but we can still enjoy the taste of the pickled eggs.

2 tablespoons mild prepared
  mustard
½ cup water
2 cups distilled white vinegar
1 cup sugar
1 tablespoon salt

1 tablespoon celery seed
1 tablespoon mustard seed
6 whole cloves
1 dozen hard-boiled eggs, peeled
2 onions, thinly sliced

Combine mustard and water and blend until smooth. In a sauce-pan, slowly add mustard mixture to vinegar. Add sugar, salt, cel-ery seed, mustard seed, and cloves. Bring to a boil and simmer for 10 minutes. Cool slightly.

Pack eggs and onions in a glass jar and pour vinegar mixture over them to cover. Seal and refrigerate for 10–14 days before serving. YIELD: *1 dozen*

Fiesta Eggs

Next time a hungry crowd gets together after a big party, gather everyone around in the kitchen and cook up a passel of these Fiesta Eggs for a midnight breakfast that is sure to please. For a more planned affair such as a buffet brunch, keep the eggs warm in a chafing dish and serve with Picante Sauce (Chapter 7) and hot Cheese Biscuits (Chapter 8).

1 pound cooked ham, diced
2 bell peppers, seeded and
   chopped
1 large onion, chopped
4 tablespoons butter
10 eggs

6 tablespoons light cream
1 teaspoon salt
1 teaspoon pepper
½ cup chopped pimiento
   (optional)

Sauté ham, bell peppers, and onion in butter in a large, heavy skillet over medium high heat until onion is translucent.

Break eggs into a mixing bowl and beat well. Add cream, salt, and pepper and stir until well blended.

Pour eggs into skillet over ham, peppers, and onion, add pimiento if desired, and cook over medium high heat, stirring and turning with a spatula to prevent scorching, until eggs are set and firm.   YIELD: *8–10 servings*

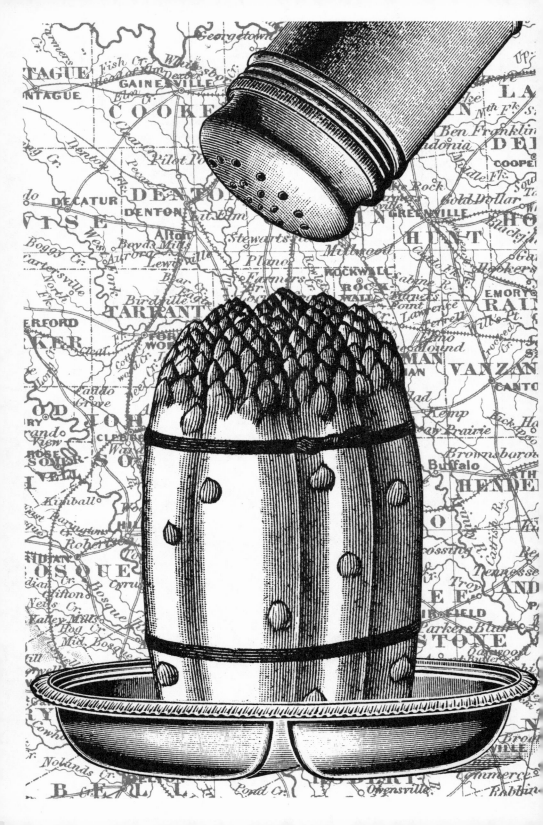

6. Vegetables and Side Dishes

Calabacitas

This recipe gets its name from the green Mexican squash which is generally used in the dish. If the Mexican variety is not available, zucchini or yellow squash can be used as well. It is an appealing dish and, with the addition of the corn, it is a true vegetable medley.

2 pounds Mexican, zucchini, or
    yellow squash (or mixture)
6 slices bacon
1 onion, chopped
2 cloves garlic, minced
2 cups chopped canned tomatoes
    with juice

½ cup water
½ teaspoon salt
½–1 cup canned or frozen corn,
    cooked and drained (optional)

Quarter and slice squash ½ inch thick. Place in a large pot with salted water to cover. Bring to a boil, cover, and reduce heat. Simmer until squash is just tender. Drain the squash and return it to pot.

Cut the bacon into small pieces. Combine bacon, chopped onion, and garlic in a large skillet and sauté over medium heat until onion is wilted and bacon begins to brown. Add chopped tomatoes (with juice), water, and salt. Cook over medium high heat about 10 minutes, until most of the liquid has reduced.

Add corn to squash (if desired) and add tomato sauce. Stir lightly, just enough to mix.   YIELD: *8 servings*

Okra Gumbo

Texas makes up a big part of the South, and we therefore claim gumbo as part of our heritage. In this classic way to prepare okra, the okra itself thickens the dish, and the tomatoes provide color as well as flavor.

4 tablespoons bacon drippings or
  oil
½ cup chopped onion
1 pound fresh okra, sliced
2 cups canned tomatoes with
  juice

¼ teaspoon sugar
½ teaspoon salt
½ teaspoon pepper

In a skillet, heat bacon drippings and sauté onion and okra over medium heat until lightly browned.

Add tomatoes and seasonings. Cover and simmer 15–20 minutes or until okra is tender.   YIELD: *4 servings*

Fried Okra

Even non–okra eaters will like this dish. It is also a hit as an appetizer when accompanied with a dip of Picante Sauce or Garlic Dressing (see recipes in Chapter 7).

2 pounds small, tender okra
½ cup cornmeal
1 cup flour
1 teaspoon baking powder

½ teaspoon salt
1 tablespoon oil
1 cup beer
oil for frying

Wash okra and drain on paper towels.

Combine cornmeal, flour, baking powder, and salt. Add 1 tablespoon oil and beer and stir until smooth.

Heat 2 inches of oil in a saucepan to 375°. Dip whole okra into batter and fry in hot oil until golden brown. Drain on a paper towel and serve immediately.   YIELD: *4–6 servings*

Chili-Cheese Casserole

This casserole, which puffs up like a soufflé, is a perfect accompaniment for grilled steaks or roasted meats. The green chilies have little "fire," but if you prefer only the delicate taste of the pepper and none of its tang, remove the seeds and membranes and rinse them in cool water before layering them in the casserole.

3 10-ounce cans whole green   4 eggs
  chilies
1½ pounds Monterrey Jack
  Cheese, grated

Drain green chilies and spread them open. In a 2-quart casserole, layer chilies and cheese, ending with cheese.

Beat eggs in a blender until foamy and pour over cheese and chilies. The casserole should be only about two-thirds full, as the mixture expands while baking.

Bake at 350° for 30–40 minutes or until the mixture is set and lightly browned. Serve immediately.   YIELD: *6–8 servings*

Stewed Tomatoes

This savory dish will bring requests for seconds even from people who pick the tomatoes out of salads, order hamburgers and say "Cut the tomato," and would not touch a grilled tomato on a bet.

Stewed Tomatoes is a particular favorite of ours, especially when it is part of one of our favorite meals: a big pot of Stewed Chicken (Chapter 5), buttered egg noodles, Stewed Tomatoes, and Dad's Pea Salad (Chapter 3) . . . heaven right here in Texas.

6 slices bacon, chopped   1 teaspoon salt
1 large onion, finely chopped   1 teaspoon black pepper
4 slices bread, cut into ½-inch   2 tablespoons sugar
  cubes
4 cups canned tomatoes with
  juice

In a large skillet, combine bacon and onion. Sauté over medium heat until bacon begins to crisp and onion is transparent. Add bread and continue cooking until bread cubes are well browned.

Add tomatoes, salt, pepper, and sugar and blend well. Cover and simmer over low heat for 20–25 minutes.

YIELD: *6–8 servings*

Lima Bean Casserole

This unusual blend of flavors makes a savory casserole to be enjoyed as a side dish with barbecue or other meats or as a main dish itself.

1 pound dried lima beans	4 cups tomato sauce
1 pound pork sausage, cut into cubes	2 cups milk
	1 cup sour cream
2 green bell peppers, chopped	2 tablespoons molasses

Wash beans. Cover with water and let soak overnight. Beans will double in bulk. Drain the beans and place in a 9-by-13-inch baking dish. Add cubed sausage and chopped peppers.

Mix tomato sauce, milk, sour cream, and molasses together and add to beans. Mix well and cover pan with foil.

Bake at 325° for 2 hours or until beans are done and most of the moisture is absorbed. Stir occasionally and add water if needed.

YIELD: *10–12 servings*

Black-Eyed Peas

Texans believe Black-Eyed Peas should be eaten on New Year's Day to assure good luck all year long. This tradition is so strong that even people who don't like them are likely to insist on eating at least a few on January 1 to start the New Year right.

3 cups dried black-eyed peas
1 medium onion, coarsely
  chopped
½ pound salt pork, cut into 1-inch
  pieces

5 cups water
salt to taste

Soak the dried peas, in water to cover, 2–4 hours or overnight.

Drain the peas and place in a large pot along with the onion and salt pork. Add 5 cups of water and bring to a boil. Lower heat, cover, and simmer for 1½ hours or until peas are tender. Add salt to taste.   YIELD: *8 servings*

Rajas

If you are fortunate enough to find fresh Poblano peppers, then this side dish deserves a try. Do not be intimidated by the word *pepper*; when the seeds and membranes are removed, only the delicate flavor remains.

6 fresh Poblano peppers

2 tablespoons vegetable oil

Wash the peppers thoroughly and dry them well. Place peppers on a baking sheet in a single layer.

Place under the broiler, under high heat, at a distance of 3–5 inches. Watching carefully, allow the peppers to blister and turn a dark brown color, turning them until they are evenly roasted.

Remove from the oven and wrap in a damp cloth or place in a large plastic bag and seal. Allow peppers to steam in bag for 15–20 minutes. Remove them from bag and peel the skins from the peppers.

At this point, you have fresh roasted and peeled green chilies.

To prepare the Rajas, remove the seeds and membranes from the inside of the roasted peppers. Slice into long, thin strips and sauté in oil.   YIELD: *4–6 servings*

Onion Rings

3 or 4 onions
1 cup flour
salt to taste

½ cup milk
oil for frying

Peel the onions and cut them into ¼-inch slices. Separate the slices into rings. Combine flour and salt and dip each ring into flour, then milk, and then flour again. Fry in hot oil (375°) until golden brown. Drain on paper towels and sprinkle with salt if desired.

YIELD: *4 servings*

Grilled Onions

A favorite Texas side dish, Grilled Onions rate right up there with French fries and Onion Rings. They are traditionally served with a pan-fried steak, such as Texas Hofbrau Steak (Chapter 4), but they are just as good on a hamburger or with pan-fried liver.

If they are to be served with steak, the onions should be grilled in the same pan used to fry the steaks. After the steaks have been cooked, grill the onions in the pan drippings. While cooking, scrape the bottom of the pan to loosen any browned pieces left from the steak.

To cook them over a campfire, place the sliced onions on aluminum foil, dot them with butter, season, and seal; place the package close to the white part of the coals, turning occasionally, and cook until the onions are tender and well browned.

Or simply prepare them as described below.

3 large onions   **salt to taste**
½–¾ cup butter or margarine

Peel and slice onions ¼–½ inch thick and separate into rings.

Melt butter or margarine in a heavy skillet over medium high heat. Add onions to the pan and toss them thoroughly so that they are all coated with butter.

When onions begin to brown, lower heat and continue cooking only until they are slightly crisp and not quite translucent. Salt to taste.   YIELD: *4–6 servings*

Baked Cheese Grits

Because of its proximity to the "Deep South," particularly its neighbor Louisiana, East Texas is quite influenced by the Southern culture. Grits is an example of this influence. This southern mainstay is ground hominy, which, when cooked, has a texture similar to cream of wheat.

Many East Texans eat grits three times a day: as a hot cereal for breakfast and as a side dish for lunch and dinner, plain or in this delicious casserole form.

6 cups water   **1 pound Cheddar cheese, grated**
2 teaspoons salt   **½ cup butter, cut in pieces**
1½ cups grits   **3 eggs**

Bring water and salt to a boil; add grits and cook about 30 minutes, until water is absorbed and mixture has a creamy texture. Remove from heat and stir in cheese, butter, and eggs. Bake in a buttered casserole dish at 350° for 75 minutes.

                                    YIELD: *8–10 servings*

Red River Cabbage

This recipe is a German variation of stir-fried cabbage. It has a tangy taste with just a hint of sweetness and a beautiful color.

½ **pound bacon**
1 large head red cabbage,
  shredded

1 cup white vinegar
4 tablespoons sugar
1 teaspoon salt

Cut bacon into small pieces and sauté over medium heat in a large pot or Dutch oven. When bacon has browned, add cabbage, a handful at a time. Toss after each addition so that all cabbage is coated with bacon drippings.

    Combine vinegar, sugar, and salt and pour over cabbage. Cover and simmer over medium heat 20–30 minutes, depending on desired crispness.   YIELD: *8 servings*

Pinto Beans

Texas has received many gifts from Mexico, and high on the list of the most prized are pinto beans. They are a staple in kitchens throughout the state—delicious, economical, high in protein, easy to prepare, and versatile. What more could one ask from a single food?

    In many Texas kitchens today, as in the past, a pot of beans is put on the stove to cook every morning. They can be prepared simply or with many creative touches. Beer can be substituted for the cooking water, and any number of fresh or dried spices can be added, such as coriander (cilantro), peppercorns, or cumin (comino). Needless to say, green chilies or jalapeños can be added, and many cooks use a little salt pork or bacon. Tomatoes and chili powder can be added, as in Ranch Beans. However they are prepared, a bowl of beans with a warm tortilla or hot cornbread is hard to surpass.

Refried beans are cooked pinto beans which are mashed and then fried in oil. Just as versatile as the whole beans, they may be eaten as a side dish, used for Chalupas, Panchos, Burritos, or Tacos, or served as a dip with tostados or chips.

Ranch Beans are the Texas adaptation of Pinto Beans and are a favorite fare for cookouts and barbecues.

The Germans had their variations as well. One of these Grandmother called Bean Soup, but it was nothing like any soup! To a pot of cooked beans she would add homemade egg noodles and some heavy cream.

Once you decide which version to cook, the cooking itself is quite simple. There are rules of thumb to follow which have been passed down through the years. The cooking vessel itself is important. If at all possible, it should be earthenware; beans are traditionally cooked in a red clay pot. Metal pans work satisfactorily, but sometimes the beans do not get as dark in color. This is a difference in appearance only and does not affect the taste. According to Mexican tradition, a pot of beans should be stirred with nothing but a wooden spoon, and salt should be added only toward the end of the cooking to avoid toughening the skins of the beans.

The cooked beans are even better the second day, as they will absorb more of the seasonings and the juice will thicken. They will remain good, refrigerated, for 5 days. They also freeze very well and can be kept frozen for up to 3 months.

Basic Pinto Beans

3 cups uncooked pinto beans
1 large onion, cut into eighths

2 cloves garlic, peeled
salt and pepper to taste

Pick and wash beans, place in a 4-quart pot, and cover with water to 2 inches above beans. Add onions and garlic.

Bring to a boil, reduce heat, and simmer 3–4 hours or until tender. Check every hour or so and add warm water as needed.

Do not stir beans during the first 2 hours of cooking. It is not necessary if there is enough water for beans to roll freely as they cook. This method produces a pot of tender beans with a nice broth.

If a thicker sauce is desired, begin stirring the beans the last hour or 2 hours of cooking and cook over medium high heat for the last hour.

Add salt and pepper to taste in the last hour of cooking.

YIELD: *12 servings*

Panhandle Baked Beans

Baked Beans are a versatile side dish and well liked by all, at cookouts or indoors. From early cowboy days to the present, the canned variety has been a staple out on the range, sometimes eaten cold, right out of the can. You will find this recipe to be far tastier than those.

This recipe should be prepared a day ahead of time, so that the beans have a chance to absorb all the delicious flavors in the sauce.

1 pound dried navy beans	2 teaspoons cider vinegar
1 onion, sliced	2 tablespoons molasses
½ teaspoon salt	2 tablespoons prepared mustard
6 ounces tomato paste	1 tablespoon Worcestershire
2 tablespoons flour	sauce
3 cups water	1 teaspoon salt
¾ cup brown sugar	10 slices bacon, chopped
½ cup catsup	½ cup chopped onion

Pick over and wash beans; cover with water and let stand overnight. Drain, rinse, and cover with fresh water. Add sliced onion and ½ teaspoon salt and cook slowly for 1 hour or until tender. Drain and set aside.

In a large saucepan, combine tomato paste and flour, blending until smooth. Slowly stir in 3 cups water. Add brown sugar, catsup, vinegar, molasses, mustard, Worcestershire sauce, and 1 teaspoon salt. Bring to a boil and remove from heat.

In a small skillet, fry bacon and onion over medium heat until bacon is lightly browned but not crisp and drain off all grease.

Add tomato mixture and bacon and onion mixture to beans and stir until well blended. Cover and refrigerate overnight or several days.

Bake at 300° for 2 hours.   YIELD: *8 servings*

Refried Beans

¾–1 cup lard, bacon drippings, or oil
3 cups cooked pinto beans

salt to taste
1 cup grated cheese (optional)

In a heavy skillet, heat lard or drippings over high heat. Add beans and begin mashing them, using the back of a wooden spoon or a potato masher. Continue mashing until beans are almost but not quite smooth; some small pieces of the beans should remain. Season with salt to taste and spread evenly over the bottom of the pan.

Lower heat to medium high and continue cooking, without stirring, until beans begin to brown around the edges.

Using a spatula, roll beans in half, as you would an omelet. Roll out of pan onto serving plate. Garnish with grated cheese if desired.   YIELD: *3 cups*

Ranch Beans

3 cups uncooked pinto beans
1 large onion, finely chopped
2 cloves garlic, minced
6 ounces tomato paste
1 cup water

1 teaspoon vinegar
2–3 teaspoons chili powder
2 teaspoons sugar
salt to taste

Pick and wash beans, cover with water, and soak overnight. Drain beans and place in a 4-quart pot. Add fresh water to 2 inches above beans. Add onion and garlic and bring to a boil. Lower heat and simmer until beans are tender, 2–3 hours. Stir occasionally, adding more water as necessary.

Combine tomato paste, 1 cup water, and vinegar and stir until well blended. Add chili powder and sugar and mix until smooth.

Pour tomato mixture into beans. Simmer over low heat, stirring occasionally, 2–3 more hours or until juice begins to thicken.

Season to taste with salt and serve.   YIELD: *12 servings*

Hot Potato Salad

Your cold cuts never had such a partner. This unique potato salad will win you over with its mixture of piquant and sweet flavors.

4 large potatoes
½ cup chopped onion
4 slices bacon, chopped
2 medium dill pickles, chopped
½ cup mayonnaise
¼ cup vinegar

¼ cup milk or cream
1 teaspoon salt
½ teaspoon sugar
½ teaspoon pepper
1 teaspoon prepared mustard

Peel and quarter potatoes and cook in a large saucepan with just enough boiling water to cover, until tender—about 20 minutes. Drain well and break up with a wooden spoon, leaving potatoes in small chunks. Set side.

Sauté onion and bacon over medium heat until browned. Remove from heat and stir in pickles, mayonnaise, vinegar, milk or cream, and seasonings. Pour over warm potatoes, mix well, and serve.   YIELD: *4–6 servings*

German Pan-Fried Potatoes

Once you have made these, it is hard to stop eating them. The flavor is fantastic, and the paprika gives the potatoes a wonderful color. Even washing the pan is a pleasure—before doing so, one can nibble on the browned pieces that are left.

6 medium potatoes, peeled
1 large onion
2 teaspoons paprika
1½ teaspoons salt

1½ teaspoons pepper
4 tablespoons bacon drippings (oil
  may be substituted)

Thinly slice potatoes and onions and spread out on paper towels to dry.

Combine paprika, salt, and pepper and sprinkle over potatoes and onions.

In a heavy skillet heat bacon drippings over medium high heat. Add potatoes and onions and stir, using a spatula to prevent potatoes from breaking up and sticking. Cook, stirring occasionally, 20–30 minutes, until potatoes are tender and well browned.

YIELD: *6–8 servings*

Potato Pancakes

The potato was held in high esteem by the German settlers in Texas, for it was a main staple in their diet. They found soon after arriving that it would grow well in Texas soil, and today it is one of the state's major truck crops.

The potato was prepared in many ways, and the Potato Pancakes are a good example. They are even better when topped with warm applesauce.

6 medium potatoes
ice water
3 eggs, beaten
1 small onion, grated

¾ cup flour
2 teaspoons salt
oil for frying

Peel potatoes, grate coarsely into a bowl of ice water, and set aside.

In a mixing bowl, combine eggs, onion, flour, and salt.

Pour off all water from potatoes and spread them out on paper towels, pressing to remove as much liquid as possible. Add potatoes to egg mixture, beating until well blended.

Heat a small amount of oil in a heavy skillet over medium heat. Spoon a heaping tablespoon of batter into pan and spread to make a 3-or-4-inch circle. Brown slowly on one side and flip. Brown the other side, pressing the pancake down with a spatula to flatten. Remove from pan and drain on paper towels. Repeat until all batter is used. YIELD: *1 dozen*

Ranch-Fried Potatoes

Some say that these are at their best when prepared in a big, black cast iron frying pan over an open fire. In any case, once you have tried them, you will be ready to switch from French fries to Ranch Fries. Serve them with grilled meats, Texas Hofbrau Steak (Chapter 4), sandwiches, or eggs.

6 medium potatoes	**oil for frying**
ice water	**salt**

Cut unpeeled potatoes into eighths. Place in a bowl, cover with ice water, and allow to stand for 30–60 minutes.

Heat ½ inch oil in heavy skillet over high heat. Remove potatoes from water and drain on paper towels. Place 8–10 potato pieces in hot oil. Fry for 1 minute, turning several times. Reduce heat to medium high and fry until golden brown and tender. Drain on paper towels and lightly salt. Reheat oil and continue process until all potatoes are fried. YIELD: *4–6 servings*

Hash Browns

Hash Browns are a side dish that can be a part of breakfast, brunch, lunch, dinner, or a midnight supper. For "Red-Hot" Hash Browns, add 1–2 teaspoons of chili powder when combining the potatoes, onion, and seasonings, and proceed as directed.

4 large potatoes	3 tablespoons butter
½ cup chopped onion	3 tablespoons bacon drippings or
1 teaspoon salt	vegetable oil
dash of pepper	

Cook potatoes, in boiling water to cover, until tender (20–30 minutes). Drain, peel, and coarsely grate. The potatoes should yield about 4 cups.

Combine grated potatoes, onion, salt, and pepper. Heat 2 tablespoons butter and 2 tablespoons bacon drippings in a heavy 10-inch skillet over medium heat. Add potato mixture, spreading evenly over the bottom of the skillet. Press the potatoes down with a spatula and cook until the bottom is browned and crusty. Slide out of the pan, intact, to a large plate.

Heat remaining butter and drippings in skillet. Slide potatoes back into pan with the unbrowned side down. Press down with a spatula again and continue cooking until the other side is browned and crusty.

Slide out to serving plate and serve immediately.

YIELD: *4 servings*

Candied Yams

Yams or sweet potatoes (they are interchangeable) are a major crop in Texas. They are plentiful and economical and a side dish Texans enjoy often. They are delicious when baked just like a white potato, but for something special the candied yams are delightful. They go extremely well with pork and, with all the variations, there is no need to save them for Thanksgiving alone.

6 large yams or sweet potatoes ⅔ **cup butter**
1 cup liquid from cooked yams   **1⅓ cups brown sugar**

Peel yams, cut into 6 or 8 pieces each, and place in a large saucepan. Add enough water to cover and bring to a boil. Cover, lower
heat, and simmer 20–30 minutes, until fork tender.

Drain yams, reserving 1 cup of the liquid.

Layer yam pieces in a 9-by-13-inch buttered baking dish and set
aside.

Combine the reserved 1 cup liquid with butter and brown sugar
in a saucepan. Bring to a boil and continue cooking over medium
high heat 3–5 minutes, until sauce begins to thicken and is
reduced.

Pour thickened sauce over yams and bake, uncovered, at 350°
for 25–30 minutes, basting once or twice.

YIELD: *10–12 servings*

VARIATIONS

Spiced Yams. Reduce the brown sugar to 1 cup. Sprinkle the yams
with a mixture of ½ cup sugar and ¼ teaspoon cinnamon before
baking.

Pineapple Yams. Substitute 1 cup pineapple juice for reserved
cooking liquid and sprinkle 1 cup crushed, drained pineapple on top
before baking.

Praline Candied Yams. Add 1 cup finely chopped pecans to the
brown sugar mixture.

Marshmallow Yams. Three to five minutes before yams are done,
cover with miniature marshmallows and return to oven. Continue
cooking until marshmallows are a golden brown.

Rice Dressing

Rice is one of the major crops grown in Texas. It thrives in the coastal lands along the Gulf of Mexico, particularly around the Houston-Galveston area. Because it is so plentiful, it is a common Texas side dish, either simply boiled and buttered or prepared with an ethnic touch. From Mexican Rice (see following recipe) to German Rice Pudding (Chapter 10), it is a statewide favorite in one form or another. This Rice Dressing has a Southern influence with a delightfully different taste.

8 cups cooked rice
½ pound pork sausage
½ pound ground beef

salt and pepper to taste
½–1 cup chicken stock

In a large skillet over medium heat, brown together rice, sausage, and beef; drain off fat. Season to taste. Add enough chicken stock to bind it together.   YIELD: *8 servings*

Mexican Rice

When you go into a restaurant in Texas and order a Mexican dinner, whether it is the Special #2 or a Fiesta Platter, there is one thing you can count on: Mexican Rice will almost always be on the plate. But don't save it just for a Mexican dinner. Try it with poultry, fish, or meat for a colorful change-of-pace side dish.

5 tablespoons bacon drippings (oil may be substituted)
1 onion, chopped
2 cloves garlic, minced
2 cups long grain rice (uncooked)
2 cups canned tomatoes (or canned tomatoes and green chilies) with juice

2 cups chicken stock (or water)
1 cup canned peas, drained (optional)
salt to taste

In a large skillet, heat bacon drippings over medium heat. Sauté onion, garlic, and rice in drippings, stirring constantly until rice is golden brown.

Break up tomatoes into small pieces, or process in blender if preferred. Add tomatoes and their juice and chicken stock to the rice. Stir only enough to mix.

Cover and simmer over low heat for 20–30 minutes or until rice is tender and all liquid is absorbed. Do not uncover or stir during cooking time.

To serve, fold in peas and add salt, as desired. If serving time is delayed, rice will keep for 30 minutes if it remains tightly covered.   YIELD: *8–10 servings*

Sopa de Fideo

Sopa de Fideo (not a soup, in spite of the name) is the Tex-Mex version of pasta. Similar to Mexican Rice, it is a versatile side dish and simple to prepare. Don't serve this dish with Mexican foods alone, because it also complements anything from baked chicken to grilled steaks. Of course, like most Texas food, it can be spiced up a tad. Just add from 2 tablespoons to 1 cup of chopped canned green chilies and ¡Olé! what a dish!

6 tablespoons bacon drippings or oil	**4 cups canned tomatoes with juice**
½ cup chopped onion	**2 teaspoons sugar**
10 ounces fideo or vermicelli	**1 teaspoon salt**
2 cloves garlic, minced	

Heat bacon drippings in a large skillet over medium heat. Add onion, fideo, and garlic and sauté until fideo turns a golden brown.

Lower heat and add tomatoes and their juice, breaking tomatoes into small pieces. Stir in sugar and salt.

Cover and simmer for 20–30 minutes or until all liquid is absorbed and fideo is tender.   YIELD: *8–10 servings*

Spoonbread

No, you do not cut it into squares and eat it like bread; you spoon it out and eat it with a fork, topping it with butter, gravy, honey, or molasses.

3 cups milk
1 cup cornmeal
1 teaspoon salt
1 teaspoon sugar

2 teaspoons baking powder
2 tablespoons butter
3 eggs, beaten

In a large saucepan, scald the milk. Gradually add the cornmeal, stirring constantly, and cook it slowly for about 10 minutes. (Mixture will become quite thick.) Remove from heat and stir in salt, sugar, baking powder, and butter. Beat the eggs and add to the cornmeal mixture, mixing well.

Pour into a buttered 1½-quart casserole and bake at 375° for 40–45 minutes. YIELD: *6–8 servings*

Roasted Corn

Put some steaks on the grill; add the corn; place some onions down in the coals (see recipe for Grilled Onions); then sit back and relax by the pool while your entire meal cooks. When it is done, add a green salad and you have a simple, yet perfect, summer barbecue without a single pan to clean.

6 ears of corn (in husks)
butter

salt and pepper to taste

Turn back several sections of the husk, being careful to leave husk intact. Remove the silk from the corn and replace the husk.

Place the corn directly on the grill over a medium charcoal fire or on a gas grill. Cook for 30–40 minutes, turning every 10 minutes or so, until husks are browned and dry.

To serve, remove husk, spread corn with butter, and sprinkle with salt and pepper. YIELD: *6 servings*

Corn Pudding

Long before the Spaniards or Mexicans inhabited Texas, the Indians roamed its plains, coastline, and mountain regions. Today, the Alabama-Coushatta tribe has a reservation near Houston which is a major tourist attraction. The Indian influence is still felt in many ways in Texas, and this recipe is an example.

Naturally, the Indians didn't use a buttered casserole dish or place it in a pan of water, but a facsimile of this corn pudding was surely baked in an adobe oven or over an open fire several hundred years ago. The Indians also didn't use canned corn, but if you are in a pinch, it will do.

As Corn Pudding has come down through the years, many variations have been made. Our German ancestors would have you sprinkle a little cinnamon or nutmeg on the top.

4 tablespoons butter	2 teaspoons sugar
2 tablespoons flour	½ teaspoon salt
1 cup milk	⅛ teaspoon pepper
2 eggs, beaten	
2 cups corn, cooked and cut from the cob	

In a large saucepan, over medium heat, melt butter and stir in flour. Gradually add milk, stirring constantly until thickened (3–5 minutes). Remove from heat and add beaten eggs, stirring with a wire whisk.

Stir in corn, sugar, salt, and pepper and pour into a buttered 1½-quart casserole. Place casserole in a shallow pan half-filled with warm water.

Bake at 350° for 45 minutes or until pudding is set.

YIELD: *4–6 servings*

Cornbread Dressing

Each area of the country has its own special touch to make holiday poultry stuffing unique. Texans use cornbread to impart a delicious flavor. But cornbread is only the beginning; in our family alone there are numerous variations. To make sure that everyone's favorite is on the holiday table, three or four varieties are usually made. One kind is used to stuff the bird and the rest made in separate casseroles.

The basic recipe is used for starters and then the creativity begins. The turkey giblets can be boiled, diced, and added along with or instead of the sausage. Finely chopped apples (1–2 cups) may be added during the last mixing, as well as 1 cup of chopped pecans or walnuts.

With the use of a food processor, the work is cut to a minimum, so double the recipe and freeze some for up to 2 months to enjoy later.

2 cups finely chopped celery
1–1½ cups finely chopped onion
½ cup butter
6 cups stale dry bread crumbs
6 cups dry cornbread crumbs
3–4 cups warm chicken stock (or water)

½ pound pork sausage
2 eggs, well beaten
salt and pepper to taste
½ teaspoon sage
4 tablespoons butter

In a large skillet over medium heat, sauté celery and onions in ½ cup butter and set aside.

Combine breads in a large mixing bowl. Pour chicken stock (or water) over bread and toss to moisten. Add celery and onions.

In the same skillet, cook sausage over medium heat until it is browned and crumbly; drain well.

Add sausage and beaten eggs to bread mixture. Add seasoning and mix well. Taste the dressing at this point and correct seasoning if necessary.

Use to stuff poultry or turn mixture into a buttered 3-quart casserole or 9-by-13-inch baking pan and lightly pat down to compress and smooth top. Dot with 4 tablespoons butter. Bake at 350° for 45–60 minutes or until a light brown crust begins to form around edges.   YIELD: *18–20 servings*

7. Salad Dressings, Gravies, and Sauces

Ranch Dressing

This is a smooth buttermilk dressing that can be kept on hand for several weeks. Use it for salads, and for an extra touch sprinkle grated Cheddar cheese on top. It is also a big hit as an appetizer, surrounded by mounds of fresh vegetables for dipping, or as a topping for baked potatoes.

1 cup buttermilk
2 cups mayonnaise
1 teaspoon grated onion
1 tablespoon finely chopped
   parsley

1 clove garlic, finely minced
½–1 teaspoon salt
pepper to taste

Slowly stir buttermilk into mayonnaise, using a fork or wire whisk. Add remaining ingredients and stir until well blended.
   Cover and refrigerate for several hours before using.

YIELD: *3 cups*

Garlic Dressing

For garlic-lovers only . . .

2 cups mayonnaise
¾ cup oil
¼ cup vinegar

½ teaspoon salt
4–5 cloves garlic, pressed

Place mayonnaise in a mixing bowl. Combine remaining ingredients. Gradually add to the mayonnaise, beating constantly with a wire whisk.

Place in a jar and refrigerate overnight. The dressing thickens as it chills. YIELD: *3 cups*

Poppyseed Dressing

A nation-wide favorite, particularly enjoyed by Texans when spooned over sections of Ruby Red grapefruit (from the Rio Grande Valley, of course) and avocado slices.

1 small onion	⅓ cup vinegar
⅓ cup sugar	1 cup vegetable oil
1 teaspoon dry mustard	1½ tablespoons poppyseeds
1 teaspoon salt	

Blend onion in a blender; remove juice and pulp and strain to produce 1–1½ tablespoons onion juice. Return juice to blender and add sugar, mustard, salt, and vinegar. Blend to combine. Continue blending while slowly adding the oil. Remove from blender and stir in the poppyseeds.

Store in the refrigerator for up to 2 weeks. YIELD: *1½ cups*

Avocado Dressing

The beautiful color of this dressing alone would enhance any salad, and it tastes as good as it looks. It is wonderful on green or vegetable salads, and it makes a delicious dressing for fruit if the garlic is omitted.

2 ripe avocados	1 clove garlic, minced
3 tablespoons lemon juice	¼ cup mayonnaise
1 tablespoon grated onion	¼ cup sour cream
½ teaspoon salt	dash of Tabasco sauce

Peel and seed avocados. Place in a blender with the lemon juice and puree. Add remaining ingredients and blend until smooth and creamy. If dressing is too thick, thin with milk to desired consistency.   YIELD: *1½ cups*

Brown Gravy

There are some things that just would not be the same without gravy, and this Brown Gravy is one of the best. Using cornstarch as a thickening agent gives it a translucent appearance.

2 tablespoons grease from pan drippings	2 tablespoons cornstarch
2 cups liquid—water and pan juice	¼ cup cold water
	salt and pepper to taste

After roasting beef or pork, pour off all but 2 tablespoons grease from pan, reserving any juice left from roast. Add water to the juice to equal 2 cups. Return to pan and cook over medium heat, scraping pan to loosen drippings.

Combine cornstarch with ¼ cup cold water to make a smooth paste. Gradually pour into pan, stirring constantly until thickened. Season to taste and serve.   YIELD: *2 cups*

Cream Gravy

This is really southern-style gravy. It is probably known best as the finishing touch on Chicken-Fried Steak (Chapter 4) and mashed potatoes. However, split open a hot biscuit and spoon on the gravy and you will be enjoying an eating tradition from the olden days. Cream Gravy and biscuits were almost always on the frontier table and could make a meal stretch if unexpected guests arrived for breakfast, lunch, or dinner.

3 tablespoons pan drippings	1 cup water
3 tablespoons flour	salt and pepper to taste
1 cup evaporated milk	

After frying chicken, chicken-fried steak, or pork chops, pour off all but 3 tablespoons oil from pan. Loosen any browned pieces from the bottom of the pan and add flour. Combine flour and drippings and stir until smooth.

Combine evaporated milk and water. With pan over medium heat, gradually add milk mixture, stirring constantly until thickened. Scrape sides and bottom to loosen any more browned pieces.

Correct seasoning. YIELD: *2½–3 cups*

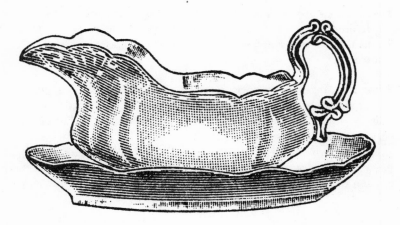

Barbecue Sauces

The following barbecue sauces, coming from Dad and his Dad before him, have passed the test of time. One of them is sure to enhance anything you decide to throw on the grill.

Remember that the sauce is an integral part of the barbecue process and can be as important as the cut of meat it flavors. For more hints on basting and sauces, refer to the information under Texas Style Barbecue in Chapter 4.

Basting Sauce for Barbecue

1 cup butter or margarine (or ½
cup bacon drippings and ½ cup
butter)
4 tablespoons lemon juice
1 tablespoon Worcestershire
sauce

1 teaspoon salt
1 teaspoon black pepper
1 teaspoon garlic powder
1–2 teaspoons chili powder
2 cups water

In a saucepan, combine butter, lemon juice, Worcestershire sauce, salt, pepper, and garlic powder. Cook over low heat until butter melts.

Dissolve chili powder in water and add to butter mixture. Bring to a boil and continue cooking for 5–10 minutes.

Use as a baste for any meat, fowl, or game, basting at 20–30 minute intervals or as needed.   YIELD: *3–4 cups*

Harvey's Barbecue Sauce

4 tablespoons bacon drippings
1 cup catsup
½ cup unsulfured molasses
¼ cup vinegar

2 tablespoons chili powder
1 teaspoon dry mustard
½ teaspoon salt
½ teaspoon cayenne pepper

2 tablespoons Worcestershire
  sauce
1 cup chicken or beef stock (or
  water)

½ teaspoon garlic powder
1½ cups water

In a heavy saucepan, combine bacon drippings, catsup, molasses, vinegar, and Worcestershire sauce and begin cooking over medium heat. Stir in stock.

In a small bowl, combine dry ingredients, mixing until well blended. Slowly add 1½ cups water, mix until smooth, and add to the catsup mixture.

Bring sauce to a boil and boil vigorously for 10 minutes. Reduce heat, cover, and simmer for 45–50 minutes.

Allow to cool and stand at room temperature for 1½–2 hours. When ready to serve, reheat. Any leftover sauce will keep in the refrigerator for 2–3 weeks.　　　　YIELD: *1 quart*

Five-Star Barbecue Sauce

4 tablespoons bacon drippings or
  oil
1 cup finely chopped onion
4 cloves garlic, minced
4 cups tomato sauce
2 tablespoons lemon juice
4 tablespoons brown sugar
2 packets unflavored gelatin
¾ cup cold water

1½ tablespoons powdered beef
  bouillon
¾ cup hot water
1 tablespoon natural smoke flavoring (optional)
¾ teaspoon salt
½ teaspoon cayenne pepper
½ teaspoon cinnamon
½ teaspoon nutmeg

Combine bacon drippings or oil, onion, and garlic in heavy saucepan and sauté over medium heat until onion and garlic are lightly browned. Stir in tomato sauce, lemon juice, and brown sugar.

Dissolve gelatin in cold water, bouillon in hot water. Add both to tomato sauce mixture, along with smoke flavoring (if desired), salt, cayenne, cinnamon, and nutmeg, and boil vigorously for 10 minutes. Reduce heat, cover, and simmer slowly for an additional 45–50 minutes, stirring occasionally.

Allow sauce to cool and stand at room temperature for 1½–2 hours before serving to allow flavors to blend. When ready to use, reheat and serve over barbecued chicken or pork.

YIELD: *2½ pints*

Cocktail Sauce

A standard with seafood, this sauce is particularly enjoyed with "peel your own" fresh Gulf shrimp, as in Shrimp Boiled in Beer (Chapter 5).

1 cup catsup
3–4 tablespoons lemon juice
1 teaspoon prepared horseradish

2 teaspoons Worcestershire sauce
2 or 3 drops Tabasco sauce
  (optional)

Combine all ingredients and blend until smooth. YIELD: *1½ cups*

Hot Sauces

Texans probably eat as much "hot sauce" as they drink beer, and there are those who say that the two go hand in hand. The big misconception is that hot sauce must be of the five-alarm variety, burning all the way down your throat and in the pit of your stomach. But that is not necessarily so. In fact, when the sauce is spiced to that degree, many of its wonderful flavors are entirely missed.

It is true, though, that some form of hot sauce is on many tables right along with the salt and pepper. Rumor has it that Texans put it on everything they eat. That may be close, although it is doubtful that it has been used to top an ice cream sundae.

All rumors and hearsay aside, hot sauce definitely enhances many foods. It can always be made in varying degrees of spiciness to suit almost any tastebud. The recipes here are a sampling of the many varieties of sauces which are prepared or are available all over the state. One of them is bound to be right for you.

Picante Sauce

2 cups canned tomatoes with
  juice
1 small onion

2–4 fresh Serrano peppers
pinch of sugar
salt to taste

Place all ingredients in a blender or food processor and blend until
finely chopped.
    Pour into a saucepan and bring to a boil. Lower heat and sim-
mer for 30 minutes. Cool slightly, poor into a pint jar, seal, and
refrigerate.
    This sauce will keep 3–4 weeks in the refrigerator. YIELD: *2 cups*

Fresh Mexican Salsa

1 cup chopped tomato
¼ cup chopped onion
1 tablespoon fresh coriander
  (cilantro), finely chopped

2–3 fresh Serrano peppers,
  minced
½ teaspoon salt
2–4 tablespoons water

Combine tomato, onion, coriander, and peppers, add salt, and mix
well. Add 2–4 tablespoons water, depending on juiciness of
tomatoes.
    This sauce is best used immediately. However, it can be made up
to 3 hours ahead if need be. YIELD: *1½–2 cups*

Green Tomato Sauce

2 cups cooked green tomatoes
1 clove garlic
¼ cup chopped onion
2–3 fresh Serrano peppers
1 tablespoon fresh coriander
  (cilantro), chopped (optional)

pinch of sugar
salt to taste
1 tablespoon vegetable oil

Combined all ingredients except oil in a blender and process just until blended.

In a small skillet, heat the oil and pour in the tomato mixture. Bring to a boil and simmer 3–5 minutes. Allow to cool and refrigerate.

This sauce will keep up to 2 weeks in the refrigerator.

YIELD: *2 cups*

Hot Sauce

4 large tomatoes
2–3 fresh jalapeño peppers
1 small onion
2 cloves garlic

2 teaspoons fresh coriander
  (cilantro) (optional)
1 teaspoon salt
1–2 tablespoons water

In a blender or food processor, combine 1 tomato, the jalapeños, onion, garlic, and coriander. Blend or process until finely chopped. Add remaining tomatoes and blend only until finely chopped. Do not puree or overblend.

Add salt and 1–2 tablespoons water, depending on the juiciness of tomatoes.

The sauce will keep in the refrigerator for up to 1 week.

YIELD: *2 cups*

Lemon Sauce

Grandma's gingerbread (see Three Rivers Gingerbread, Chapter 10) was always a treat, and when she made Lemon Sauce to top it, we knew it was a special night. This delicate sauce also complements Bread Pudding or 1-2-3-4 Cake (Chapter 10).

2 tablespoons cornstarch
1 cup sugar
1½ cups water
½ cup lemon juice

4 tablespoons butter
1–2 teaspoons grated lemon rind
  (optional)

In a small saucepan, combine cornstarch and sugar and blend well. Slowly add water and lemon juice, stirring until smooth. Bring to a boil over medium high heat, stirring constantly. Lower heat and continue cooking 2–3 minutes or until thickened. Remove from heat and stir in butter and lemon rind, if desired. Serve warm.

YIELD: *3 cups*

Custard Sauce

The richness of a custard filling and a creamy, thick texture combine to make this sauce a delightful topping for fresh strawberries or peaches or Bread Pudding (Chapter 10).

3 eggs, beaten
⅓–½ cup sugar
pinch of salt

2½ cups milk
1 teaspoon vanilla

Combine eggs, sugar, and salt in the top of a double-boiler and blend well.

Gradualy add milk, and cook over hot, not boiling, water, stirring constantly, until mixture begins to thicken (about 20 minutes).

Remove from heat and stir in vanilla. Cool and chill for several hours.

YIELD: *3 cups*

Mom's Hot Fudge Sauce

Hot Fudge Sauce is a chocolate lover's dream. In our childhood, when Mom made the sauce, we would get in line with our bowls of ice cream. Those who liked a regular fudge sauce were first in line. When they had been served, Mom would boil the sauce an additional minute or two, so that when it hit the cold ice cream it got hard and chewy. Those of us at the end of the line had to have more patience, but it was well worth the wait.

1 cup sugar
2 tablespoons cocoa
¼ cup water

1 tablespoon butter
½ teaspoon vanilla

In a small saucepan, combine sugar and cocoa. Gradually add water and bring to a boil over medium heat. Stir constantly and continue boiling for 1 minute. Remove from heat and stir in butter and vanilla.   YIELD: *1½ cups (4 to 6 servings)*

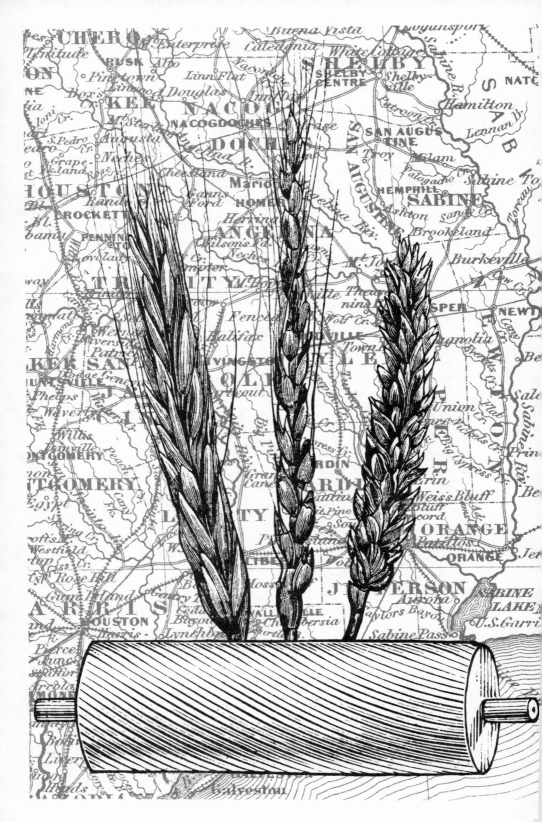

8. Breads

Biscuits

Cowboys of the past were a pretty healthy breed in spite of their diet, which consisted mostly of fried meats and biscuits. Biscuits were a mainstay of life then, from the rock-hard variety carried in saddlebags to the more edible variety turned out by the chuckwagon boss. Fortunately, biscuits have come a long way since then.

2 cups sifted flour
3 teaspoons baking powder
1 teaspoon salt

⅓ cup shortening
¾ cup milk

Sift flour, baking powder, and salt together. Using a pastry cutter or two knives, cut shortening into dry ingredients until mixture has the texture of coarse meal.

Slowly add milk, mixing to form a smooth dough. Turn out onto a floured board and knead lightly. Roll out to ½-inch thickness and cut with a floured 2-inch biscuit cutter.

Transfer biscuits to an ungreased baking sheet and bake at 450° for 10–12 minutes or until lightly browned.   YIELD: *1 dozen*

VARIATIONS

Drop Biscuits. Add up to 1 cup milk to ingredients. Do not knead. Drop by heaping tablespoons onto baking sheets and bake as above.

Cheese Biscuits. Add ½ cup grated Cheddar cheese to dough just before kneading. Proceed as directed above.

Bacon or Ham Biscuits. Add ⅓ cup crumbled, fried bacon or ⅓ cup finely diced ham to dough just before kneading.

Raised Buttermilk Biscuits

5 cups flour	¾ cup shortening
3 teaspoons baking powder	1 tablespoon (1 package) dry
1 teaspoon salt	yeast
1 teaspoon baking soda	¼ cup lukewarm water
4 tablespoons sugar	2 cups buttermilk

Sift flour, baking powder, salt, soda, and sugar together and cut in shortening. In a large bowl, dissolve yeast in lukewarm water and add buttermilk. Gradually add dry ingredients, mixing well, until all the flour mixture is moistened. Cover and refrigerate overnight or for up to 2 weeks.

When ready to use, take out desired amount of dough. Roll out on a floured board to ½-inch thickness. Cut with a 2-inch biscuit cutter and place biscuits 2 inches apart on a greased cookie sheet. Grease the top of each biscuit and set aside to rise for 1 hour.

Bake at 400° for 10–15 minutes.   YIELD: *4–5 dozen*

Buckwheat Cakes

These are hotcakes with a buckwheat flavor and are traditionally served with molasses, but they are also good with honey, syrup, or a fruit sauce.

1 cup buckwheat flour	½ teaspoon salt
1 cup white flour	3 cups buttermilk
1 teaspoon baking powder	¼ cup vegetable oil
1½ teaspoons soda	

Combine dry ingredients and add buttermilk and oil. Stir only until dry ingredients are moistened. The batter should be thin. Add more buttermilk, if necessary.

Grease and heat a large griddle. Pour ¼ cup batter on heated griddle for each cake. Cook on one side until bubbles form on top. Flip and cook other side until browned. Stir down batter before using each time.   YIELD: *1½–2 dozen*

Monkey Bread

There is nothing like freshly baked yeast bread, especially when it is baked in your own kitchen. The aroma of the yeast drifts all through the house and seems to say "welcome" to all who come through the door. This bread comes out of the oven already buttered and ready to pull apart and enjoy. Vary this by rolling the buttered balls in herbs, cheese, or cinnamon and sugar before baking.

¾ **cup milk**
4 tablespoons butter
4 tablespoons sugar
1 teaspoon salt

1 tablespoon (1 package) dry
  yeast
3–3½ cups flour
½ cup melted butter

In a small saucepan, scald milk and add the 4 tablespoons butter, sugar, and salt. Cook milk mixture to 115–120°.

Combine yeast and milk mixture in a large bowl and stir until yeast is dissolved.

Gradually add flour and mix until a soft dough is formed. No kneading is necessary. Place in a buttered bowl, cover, and let rise in a warm place until doubled—about an hour.

Punch down the dough and turn out onto a lightly floured board. Roll dough to ½-inch thickness. Cut into 1-inch squares.

Dip each square into the ½ cup melted butter. Layer the squares in a 10-inch tube pan. Let rise until doubled again—30–40 minutes.

Bake at 425° for 10 minutes. Reduce heat to 375° and continue baking for an additional 20–30 minutes.

If the bread browns too quickly, cover with foil. When done, unmold and serve immediately.   YIELD: *1 loaf*

Bolillos

Bolillos are a wonderful Mexican yeast roll. They have a hard outer crust much like French bread, but the inside is moist, dense, and rich in yeast flavor. Anyone who has tried them knows that it would be easy to become addicted to them—hot or cold! In Mexico they are offered at three meals a day because once you have had them for breakfast you cannot wait to have them for lunch and dinner, too.

1 tablespoon (1 package) dry yeast	**2 teaspoons sugar**
	6 cups flour
1 tablespoon salt	**2 cups hot water**

In a large bowl, combine yeast, salt, sugar, and 2 cups flour. Add the hot water and blend until all the flour is moistened. Add remaining flour, 1 cup at a time.

Turn dough onto a lightly floured board and knead for 10–15 minutes or until the dough is smooth and elastic. If dough becomes sticky, add more flour as needed.

Place the dough in a greased bowl and grease the top of the dough. Cover and let rise until doubled, about 1½ hours.

When doubled in size, punch down the dough and divide into 20–24 even ball-shaped pieces. Form each piece into an oblong shape with the center thicker than the ends.

Place the Bolillos on a greased baking sheet about 2 inches apart. Cover and allow to rise again until doubled in size, about 30–45 minutes.

Before baking, cut a slash lengthwise along each roll, using a sharp knife or razor blade.

Bake at 400° for 10 minutes, then reduce heat to 350° and continue baking for 20 minutes or until the loaves are golden and sound hollow when tapped.   YIELD: *20–24*

Tortillas

Tortillas, the basic bread-food of Mexicans and Texans, are the most versatile of all breads. These round, flat discs, made of corn masa or wheat flour, are used as an ingredient or wrapper for foods served from breakfast through dinner.

Though tortillas are readily available in markets or specialty stores, they are not as good as the handmade version.

Flour Tortillas

3 cups flour
3 teaspoons baking powder
1 teaspoon salt

4 tablespoons vegetable oil
1 cup warm water

Combine flour, baking powder, salt, and oil in a mixing bowl. Add water and mix until well blended. Turn out on a floured board and knead 3–5 minutes until soft and no longer sticky. Cover dough and allow it to rest for 20–30 minutes.

Roll dough into balls about 1½ inches in diameter. Return balls to mixing bowl and cover with a damp cloth. On a floured board, roll out one ball with a rolling pin into a circle about 6 inches in diameter and ¼ inch thick.

Cook on a hot ungreased griddle until lightly browned on both sides. Continue until all the dough is used. As tortillas are done, place in a cloth-lined basket or bowl and cover to keep warm and moist.   YIELD: *16–18*

Corn Tortillas

2 cups masa harina   **1 cup water**

In a small bowl, combine masa and water and mix until dough forms a ball. If mixture is too dry, add an additional 1–2 tablespoons water. Roll dough in balls 1½ inches in diameter. Return to bowl and cover with a damp cloth.

Place one ball between two sheets of plastic wrap or two plastic bags. Roll out with a rolling pin or press in tortilla press to form a 6-inch circle. A pie plate may also be used to flatten tortilla.

To cook tortillas, carefully peel off top bag or plastic and transfer tortilla to your hand. Peel off bottom layer of plastic and place tortilla on a hot ungreased griddle or heavy skillet. Cook for 1 minute, flip, and cook other side for another minute until browned or until tortilla begins to puff.

Remove and place in a cloth-lined bowl or basket and cover. Repeat procedure for remaining balls.   YIELD: *16–18*

Cornbread

Cornbread is a traditional southern dish that traveled to Texas with the settlers. Whether baked in a pan or fried on a skillet in cakes, it was always a favorite.

Biscuits or cornbread of some kind were served at every meal during pioneer days. Bread was a good filler when the pickings were slim as well as a complement to a well-laid table.

Because it was served so often, there were many variations of the basic cornbread recipe. Cracklin' Cornbread is a buttermilk cornbread with the added flavor and crunch of cracklings or bacon. For a delicious Buttermilk Cornbread, simply omit the cracklings or bacon from the Cracklin' Cornbread recipe. Jalapeño Cornbread is a more elaborate version and a taste treat, especially with a bowl of pinto beans. Corn Cakes are griddle cakes cooked to a golden brown with crispy edges. (See also Spoonbread, in Chapter 6.)

There are as many different baking utensils for cornbread as there are recipes. Black cast iron utensils are considered the best, and they include round skillets, cornsticks, muffin tins, and wedges.

Regardless of which recipe is used or in what shape it is baked, it is a lasting food of our past and present. There is no reason to throw any leftover cornbread away even if it is stale. The stale bread is used as Cornbread Dressing (Chapter 6), eaten crumbled in a bowl with milk poured over it, or softened by dunking it in a bowl of beans or Red-Eye Gravy (Chapter 4).

Basic Cornbread

1½ cups cornmeal	2 teaspoons sugar (optional)
½ cup flour	1 egg
2 teaspoons baking powder	¼ cup bacon drippings or oil
1 teaspoon salt	1 cup milk

Sift cornmeal, flour, baking powder, salt, and sugar together. Combine egg, bacon drippings or oil, and milk and add to flour mixture. Mix until smooth.

Pour into a greased 9-inch square pan, 10-inch skillet, or 12 muffin tins. Bake at 425° for 20–30 minutes or until golden brown.   YIELD: *6 servings*

Cracklin' Cornbread

2 cups cornmeal	2 tablespoons molasses
1 teaspoon salt	1 egg
½ teaspoon soda	1½ cups buttermilk
1 teaspoon baking powder	1½ cups cooked, crumbled crack-
½ cup flour	lings or bacon

Combine cornmeal, salt, soda, baking powder, and flour and set aside. Combine molasses, egg, and buttermilk and add to dry ingredients. Mix until just smooth. Stir in the cracklings or bacon.

Generously grease a 10-inch ovenproof skillet. Place the skillet in a 425° oven for 2–3 minutes or until it is very hot. Remove the skillet and immediately pour in the cornmeal mixture. Return it to the oven and bake at 425° for 25 minutes.

YIELD: *6–8 servings*

Jalapeño Cornbread

3 cups yellow cornmeal
3 tablespoons flour
2 teaspoons baking powder
1 teaspoon salt
2 tablespoons sugar
2½ cups milk
½ cup vegetable oil or bacon
  drippings

3 eggs, beaten
1 cup chopped onion
1 cup cream-style cooked corn
¼–½ cup finely chopped canned
  jalapeño peppers
1½ cups grated Longhorn or
  Cheddar cheese

In a large bowl, combine cornmeal, flour, baking powder, salt, and sugar. Add milk, oil or bacon drippings, and beaten eggs and mix until smooth.

Stir in onion, corn, jalapeños (to taste), and cheese. Pour into well-greased muffin tins and bake at 425° for 20–25 minutes or until lightly browned. YIELD: *2½–3 dozen*

Corn Cakes

1 cup cornmeal
½ cup boiling water
1 tablespoon flour

1 teaspoon salt
1 egg
½ cup milk

Place cornmeal in a bowl and scald it by adding the boiling water. Allow to cool slightly.

Add the remaining ingredients and mix until smooth. The batter will be quite thin.

Pour into 6-inch cakes on a hot, greased griddle over medium high heat. When the cakes are browned and crisp around the edges on one side (after 2–3 minutes), flip and cook the other side. Keep the griddle well greased as you proceed with the remaining batter.

Serve immediately with molasses, honey, or syrup.

YIELD: *1 dozen*

Hush Puppies

A fried fish dinner would not be complete without these cornmeal tidbits of Southern heritage. Fry up a batch and see how fast they disappear.

2 cups cornmeal, white or yellow	1 egg
¼ cup flour	1¼ cups buttermilk
1 teaspoon baking soda	½ cup finely chopped onion
2 teaspoons baking powder	oil for frying
1 teaspoon salt	

Combine cornmeal, flour, baking soda, baking powder, and salt and stir with a fork to mix evenly. Beat the egg; add buttermilk and chopped onion. Add to cornmeal mixture and stir only until well moistened.

Heat 1 inch of oil in a heavy skillet to 350–375°. Drop batter by teaspoonfuls into hot oil and fry until golden brown. Drain on paper towels.

YIELD: *2 dozen*

Korn Kisses

In the 1880's, railroads began to cross Texas, thus putting an end to the famous cattle drives and bringing more and more settlers to the state. Between 1900 and 1920 the miles of tracks were greatly increased. During this time and long after, several of our ancestors worked for the railroads—the Southern Pacific, the B&M, and the Katy.

It was in the dining cars of the Katy that a facsimile of this recipe originated and was passed on to us by our railroad men.

Made with white cornmeal, these delectable little tidbits come out of the oven in the shape of chocolate kisses.

4 cups milk	**1 tablespoon sugar**
½ cup butter	**1½ cups white cornmeal**

Pour milk into a large saucepan and bring to a boil. Add butter and sugar and stir until butter is melted. Continue cooking over medium heat and add cornmeal, ½ cup at a time, stirring constantly with a wire whisk. After all cornmeal has been added and mixture begins to thicken (3–5 minutes), remove from heat and allow to cool for about 5 minutes. The mixture will continue to thicken as it cools.

Place half of the cornmeal mixture in a pastry bag with a ⅜-inch tube. Squeeze out into peaked mounds about 1½ inches in diameter on an ungreased baking sheet. Continue until all batter is used.

Bake at 425° for about 20 minutes or until golden brown.

YIELD: *3 dozen*

Hill Country Peach Coffeecake

Fresh peaches and crumb topping make this easy coffeecake a delightful treat on a summer morning.

1 cup peeled, sliced peaches	**1½ teaspoons baking powder**
1 teaspoon lemon juice	**½ teaspoon salt**
1 teaspoon sugar	**½ cup milk**
½ cup butter, softened	**⅓ cup flour**
1 cup sugar	**¼ cup sugar**
1 egg	**3 tablespoons butter, softened**
1 teaspoon vanilla	**¼ cup chopped pecans**
2 cups flour	

Combine peaches, lemon juice, and 1 teaspoon sugar and set aside.
Cream butter, 1 cup sugar, and egg until light and stir in vanilla.
Sift 2 cups flour, baking powder, and salt together and add to the creamed mixture alternately with milk.
Pour into a greased and floured 9-inch square baking pan. Drain peaches and arrange on top of batter.
Combine ⅓ cup flour and ¼ cup sugar and cut in 3 tablespoons softened butter until mixture is crumbly. Add chopped pecans and sprinkle this mixture over peaches.
Bake at 350° for 1 hour.   YIELD: *6–8 servings*

German Coffeecake

The early German settlers in Texas had a tradition of eating several mini-meals during the day, one at mid-morning and one at mid-afternoon as well as their three main meals. The mid-morning meal was called a "second breakfast" and consisted of a slice of fresh bread with butter and jam, sweet rolls, or coffeecake along with coffee or sweet milk. Therefore, breads, rolls, and coffeecakes were baked fresh daily.

This coffeecake is typical of one served in those days. It is made of a sweet yeast dough, topped with pools of heavy cream, and lightly sprinkled with sugar. It is an indescribable taste treat of yesterday and today.

1 tablespoon (1 package) dry
  yeast
¼ cup warm water
1 cup milk
¼ cup butter
½ cup sugar

1 egg, beaten
½ teaspoon salt
4 cups flour
¼ cup butter, melted
2 cups heavy cream
8 tablespoons sugar

In a large bowl, dissolve yeast in warm water (115°–125°). Scald the milk and allow to cool to 115–125°. To the warm milk, add ¼ cup butter, ½ cup sugar, egg, and salt. Stir this mixture until the butter has melted. Add the milk mixture to the yeast. Add the flour, 1 cup at a time, mixing well after each addition.

Turn the dough out on a lightly floured board. Knead for 5–10 minutes, until it is smooth and no longer sticky. (Add more flour to the board as needed.)

Place the dough in a buttered bowl, cover, and let rise in a warm place until it has doubled in bulk—1½–2 hours.

After it has doubled, punch the dough down in the center and turn out on a lightly floured board. Knead for 20–30 seconds. Allow it to rest for 5–10 minutes.

Divide the dough into 4 even pieces. Roll out each piece into a circle about ¼ inch thick and 8–9 inches in diameter. Place each circle in a greased 9-inch cake pan. Cover and let rise again until doubled—45–60 minutes.

Using 2 or 3 fingers, make 8–10 indentions in each cake, leaving a ½-inch border around the edge. Brush each indention with melted butter. Pour ½ cup heavy cream over each cake. Sprinkle each one with 2 tablespoons sugar.

Bake at 375° for 25 minutes or until the dough is beginning to brown around the edges. Serve immediately.

These coffeecakes may be made a day ahead and refrigerated after the second rising. When ready to bake, allow to stand at room temperature for 15–20 minutes and then proceed with the topping and baking.   YIELD: *4 9-inch cakes*

Cinnamon Rolls

Just the kind you would find in a quaint bakery in some small Texas town—and a delight to bake in your own kitchen.

1 cup milk	4 tablespoons melted butter
¼ cup butter	1 cup sugar
¼ cup sugar	1 teaspoon cinnamon
1 teaspoon salt	1 cup raisins
1 tablespoon (1 package) dry	1 cup chopped nuts
yeast	1 cup powdered sugar
¼ cup lukewarm water	1 tablespoon milk
2 eggs, beaten	½ teaspoon vanilla
3½ cups flour	

Scald 1 cup milk in a small saucepan and add ¼ cup butter, ¼ cup sugar, and salt. Cool to lukewarm.

Dissolve yeast in ¼ cup lukewarm water, stirring until dissolved. Add milk mixture and eggs. Gradually add flour and mix until you have a soft dough. Turn out onto a floured board and knead until smooth (about 5 minutes). Place in a buttered bowl, cover, and let rise until doubled (1–1½ hours).

Punch down dough and knead for 20–30 seconds. Allow dough to rest for 10 minutes.

Roll out half of the dough into a rectangle, ¼ inch thick. Brush with melted butter. Combine 1 cup sugar, cinnamon, raisins, and nuts. Spread half of this on dough. Roll up jelly-roll fashion, beginning with long side. Place on greased baking sheet. Using a sharp knife, make cuts 1 inch apart, cutting almost, but not all the way, through the roll. Repeat with other half of dough and filling.

Cover and let rise until doubled again—about 45 minutes. Bake at 375° for 15–20 minutes or until golden brown.

Combine powdered sugar, 1 tablespoon milk, and vanilla; mix until smooth. While rolls are still warm, drizzle this sugar icing over them.   YIELD: *2*

Kolaches

This sweet yeast roll with a variety of fillings came from the Czechoslovakian communities of Texas. It has become such a standard favorite that it is even baked in some school bakeries and offered for lunchtime dessert.

2 cups milk	2 tablespoons (2 packages) dry
½ cup sugar	yeast
1 egg, beaten	6 cups flour
½ cup butter	3 cups filling (see below)
1 teaspoon salt	

In a large saucepan, scald milk and add sugar, egg, butter, and salt. Cool mixture to 115–120°.

In a large bowl, dissolve yeast in warm milk mixture.

Add flour gradually and knead to very soft dough. Cover and let rise until doubled in size—about 1 hour.

Shape dough into balls about 2 inches in diameter. Place on greased baking sheets 2 inches apart. Cover and let rise again until doubled—about 30–45 minutes.

When they have risen, make an indention in the center of each roll. Fill each with desired filling and bake at 350° for 20–25 minutes.   YIELD: *3 dozen*

APRICOT FILLING

½ pound dried apricots	¼ teaspoon lemon juice
⅓ cup sugar	1½ tablespoons butter

In a large saucepan, cover apricots with water and cook until plump and tender (about 20 minutes). Drain and place in a blender or food processor and puree.

In a saucepan, combine puree with sugar, lemon juice, and butter. Cook over medium heat until butter has melted.

YIELD: *1½ cups*

CHEESE FILLING

1½ cups cottage cheese
½ cup sugar
pinch of salt

1 egg, beaten
1 teaspoon vanilla
3 tablespoons melted butter

Squeeze cottage cheese in cheesecloth until dry. Combine cheese with remaining ingredients and mix well.   YIELD: *1½ cups*

Three Rivers Gingerbread

At the junction of the Frio, Nueces, and Atascosa rivers is a small town appropriately named Three Rivers, Texas. It was here, four generations ago, that this recipe originated, and it has been handed down since then.

Truly the kind that Grandma used to make, it will delight family and friends alike when they get the first whiff of its aroma from the oven. Serve it warm with Lemon Sauce (Chapter 7) for a special treat.

½ cup sugar
¼ cup butter, softened
¼ cup shortening
1 egg, beaten
1 cup unsulphured molasses
2½ cups flour

1½ teaspoons soda
1 teaspoon cinnamon
1 teaspoon ground ginger
1 teaspoon ground cloves
½ teaspoon salt
1 cup hot water

Combine sugar, butter, and shortening and cream until light and fluffy. Add egg and molasses and beat well.

Sift flour, soda, cinnamon, ginger, cloves, and salt together and stir into creamed mixture. Slowly add hot water, mixing well. Batter will be thin.

Pour into a greased 9-by-13-inch baking pan or into 24 muffin tins.

Bake at 350° for 30–40 minutes (20–30 minutes for muffins) or until toothpick inserted in center comes out clean.

YIELD: *1 9-by-13-inch cake or 2 dozen muffins*

Grandmother's Doughnuts

We grew up hearing the story of Grandmother Erben's washtub full of doughnuts. It seems that after school or football practice my father and his brothers would bring friends home with them, and Grandmother would greet them with a washtub filled with her homemade doughnuts. She would encourage them not to be shy and to go right ahead and finish them off, for she always said that they just weren't any good at all the next day. The story goes that the boys had no trouble polishing them off.

Today, none of us has the time or patience to make a tubful, but 3 or 4 dozen are well worth the effort. They come out tall, plump, light, airy, and will certainly spoil you as far as the store-bought varieties go. Grandmother was right: they are best eaten the same day. Like Grandmother, you will have no trouble getting rid of them.

2 tablespoons (2 packages) dry
  yeast
½ cup warm water
2 cups milk
½ cup butter
1 cup sugar
1 egg, beaten
1 teaspoon salt

7–8 cups flour
oil for frying
1 cup powdered sugar, or 1 cup
  sugar mixed with ½ teaspoon
  cinnamon, or glaze of 1 cup
  powdered sugar and 4 teaspoons milk

In a large bowl, dissolve yeast in warm water (115–125°). Scald milk and allow to cool to 115–125°. To warm milk, add butter, sugar, egg, and salt. Stir until butter has melted. Add the milk mixture to the yeast along with 3½ cups flour. Stir until well blended. Add remaining flour until you have a stiff dough.

Turn the dough out on a lightly floured board. Knead for 5–10 minutes, or until it is smooth and no longer sticky. (Add more flour to the board as needed.)

Place the dough in a large, clean bowl. Cover and let rise in a warm place until it has doubled in bulk—1½–2 hours.

After it has doubled, punch the dough down in the center and turn out onto a floured board. Knead for 20–30 seconds and allow it to rest for 5–10 minutes.

Working with half of the dough at a time, roll out to a ½-inch thickness. Cut with a floured doughnut cutter. Place the doughnuts (and holes) 1 inch apart on a greased cookie sheet and let rise again until doubled—45–60 minutes.

Heat 3 inches of oil in a large saucepan to 385°. Gently slide doughnuts into hot oil, frying only one at a time. Cook for about 30 seconds, turning once to brown evenly. Drain on paper towels.

Dust the doughnuts with powdered sugar or cinnamon-sugar mixture, or dip in glaze of powdered sugar and milk. If glazing, allow to drip on wire racks until dry.   YIELD: *3–4 dozen*

Orange Rolls

2 tablespoons (2 packages) dry
  yeast
½ cup lukewarm water
2 eggs, beaten
1 tablespoon sugar
1 teaspoon salt
1 tablespoon grated orange rind
½ cup milk

½ cup lukewarm orange juice
2 tablespoons butter, melted
4½–5 cups flour
4 tablespoons melted butter
2 cups powdered sugar
1 tablespoon grated orange rind
4 tablespoons orange juice

Dissolve yeast in lukewarm water. Combine eggs, sugar, salt, and 1 tablespoon grated rind and add to yeast mixture.

Scald milk and cool to 115–120°. Add cooled milk, ½ cup luke-warm orange juice, and 2 tablespoons melted butter to yeast mixture.

Slowly add 4½ cups flour until a soft dough forms. If dough is still sticky, knead in a small amount of additional flour.

Place dough in a large buttered bowl, cover, and allow to rise in a warm place until doubled—about 1–1¼ hours.

When dough has doubled in volume, punch down and turn out onto lightly floured board. Roll dough ½ inch thick and brush with melted butter.

Roll dough in jelly-roll fashion and slice ½ inch thick.

Place slices in greased muffin tins. Cover and allow to rise again, until doubled—about 45 minutes.

Bake at 350° for 15–20 minutes. Ice with a mixture of the powdered sugar, 1 tablespoon grated rind, and 4 tablespoons orange juice.   YIELD: *3 dozen*

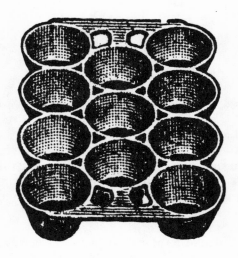

Strawberry Muffins

When you make Strawberry Shortcake (Chapter 10), you pick out the firm, beautifully shaped berries. But there are always some that are softer and not as well shaped, and these are perfect for making Strawberry Muffins. Even though these berries would not win first prize at a county fair, the delicious flavor and bright color are still there.

The muffins themselves could win a prize and are quick enough to make that they can be in the oven in the morning by the time the coffee brews.

1 cup fresh strawberries, cut into
  small pieces
½ cup brown sugar
2 cups sifted flour
¾ teaspoon soda

¼ teaspoon salt
2 eggs
½ cup milk
¼ cup vegetable oil

Combine strawberries and brown sugar and set aside. Sift flour together with soda and salt. Beat eggs and add milk and oil. Make a well in the dry ingredients and add egg mixture. Stir only until dry ingredients are moistened. Add strawberries and mix lightly.

Fill greased or papered muffin tins two-thirds full. Bake at 400° for 20–30 minutes.   YIELD: *2 dozen*

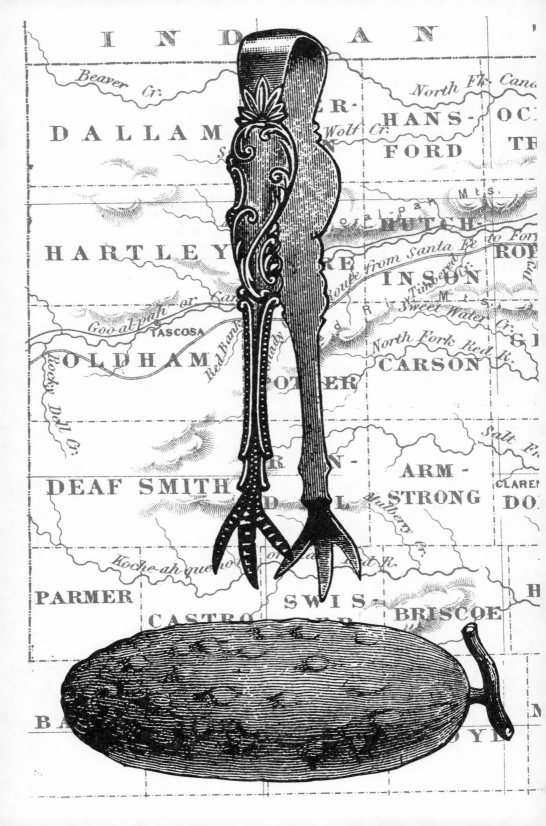

9. Pickles, Preserves, and Condiments

Fig Preserves

The abundant crop of figs in Texas allows us the luxury of putting them up into preserves.

12 cups figs, washed and quartered

6 cups sugar
2 lemons, thinly sliced

In a large saucepan, combine figs and sugar and begin cooking over low heat. Add lemons and continue cooking, stirring occasionally and skimming off any foam, for 2½–3 hours or until fruit is clear. Pour hot preserves into sterilized jars and seal immediately.

YIELD: *5–6 pints*

Strawberry Preserves

When strawberries are plentiful, make one batch of these preserves for your family to enjoy and another to put away for Christmas gift-giving.

6 cups fresh strawberries

4 cups sugar

Wash, hull, and drain strawberries. Place 3 cups strawberries in a large pan and cover with 2 cups sugar. Add remaining strawberries and sprinkle with remaining sugar. Let stand overnight, covered.

Remove strawberries and set aside. Gradually bring sugar and juice to a boil over low heat and continue boiling 3–5 minutes. Add berries and simmer an additional 20–30 minutes. Skim off any foam.

With a slotted spoon, remove berries and place in sterilized jars. Bring syrup back to a boil. Fill each jar with boiling syrup and seal immediately. YIELD: *3 pints*

Peach Preserves

What could be better on a piece of warm homemade bread than home-canned Peach Preserves?

10 cups fresh peaches, peeled and sliced   **5 cups sugar**

Combine sliced peaches and sugar in a large pan. Cook over low heat, stirring occasionally and skimming off any foam, until mixture is clear and beginning to thicken—3–4 hours. Pack in sterilized jars and seal. YIELD: *4–5 pints*

Spiced Peaches

There was always a bowl of spiced and stewed fruit on the German dinner table, and it always rounded out the meal perfectly. These Spiced Peaches are just the thing to make a hearty meal complete.

2 cups sugar
2 cups cider vinegar
2 cups water

6 sticks cinnamon
2 tablespoons whole cloves
24 fresh peaches, peeled

Combine sugar, vinegar, water, cinnamon, and cloves in a large enamel or stainless steel pan and boil for 15 minutes. Add whole peaches, one at a time, to liquid and cook over medium heat 20–30 minutes, until peaches are tender. Pack peaches into 3 sterilized quart jars. Return syrup to a boil and ladle over peaches. Be sure each jar has 2 cinnamon sticks. Seal immediately. Store in a dark place at least 2 weeks. Chill before serving.   YIELD: *3 quarts*

Pickled Pecos Cantaloupe

The small town of Pecos is located on the Pecos River in West Texas—the most arid part of the state, primarily used for cattle ranching. It is in this unlikely farming area that the gem of cantaloupes is grown—the Pecos cantaloupe. To enjoy this flavorful fruit all year, put up some Pickled Cantaloupe.

4 large cantaloupes
6 cups white vinegar
6 cups sugar

2 tablespoons pickling spice
6 cinnamon sticks

Cut cantaloupes in half, remove seeds, and peel. Cut into 1-by-2-inch pieces and place in an enamel or stainless steel pan. Cover with vinegar and let stand overnight.

Remove cantaloupe and set aside. To remaining vinegar, add sugar and pickling spice and bring to a boil. Continue cooking over high heat until syrup begins to thicken. Add melon pieces and cook over low heat 10–15 minutes. Pack cantaloupe into 6 sterilized pint jars and add 1 cinnamon stick to each. Return syrup to rapid boil and cook until reduced by half. Pour hot syrup over melon and seal immediately.   YIELD: *6 pints*

Watermelon Rind Pickles

In late spring, when the fields around Luling, Texas, are overflowing with melons, we know summer is right around the corner. In late June, when the melons reach their peak, Luling holds its annual Watermelon Thump. For the rest of the summer, roadside watermelon stands dot the countryside, and some have long picnic tables where the big, luscious melons are served by the slice.

Our Dad has always had a knack for finding the best melon. It was a special time when we would take a ride on a Sunday afternoon and stop at a watermelon stand. Dad would get out and check the melons; we would become more and more impatient as he thumped and looked around. But it was always worth the wait. We would take the chosen melon home, ice it down, and wait until he said it was time to cut it. The first peek inside told us that he had done his usual good job. We would eat all the way down to the white rind, then lift it up and drink the juice. We would probably have eaten the white part as well, but Mom always said that it would give us stomachaches. Actually, Dad wanted the rinds to make Watermelon Rind Pickles.

6 cups cubed and peeled watermelon rind
¼ cup salt
4 cups water
2 teaspoons salt

2 cups cider vinegar
2 cups sugar
1 tablespoon whole cloves
3 cinnamon sticks

Place watermelon rind in a large enamel or stainless steel pan, cover with water, and add ¼ cup salt. Cover and let stand 4–6 hours or overnight. Drain and rinse well. Return rind to enamel pan and add 4 cups water and 2 teaspoons salt. Bring to a boil, reduce heat, and simmer until just tender (15–20 minutes). Drain and set aside. Combine vinegar, sugar, and cloves in pan and boil 12–15 minutes. Add rind to vinegar mixture and cook until rind is clear—3–5 minutes. Pack rind in 3 sterilized pint jars, add 1 cinnamon stick to each jar, and ladle boiling syrup to cover. Seal immediately.   YIELD: *3 pints*

German Dill Pickles

These are easy to make, crunchy dill pickles—the perfect partner for any cold meat sandwich.

enough small pickling cucumbers to pack 6 quart jars
6 cloves garlic
18 sprigs fresh dill

2 quarts water
4 cups vinegar
1 cup salt

Wash cucumbers and pack into 6 quart jars, adding one clove of garlic and 3 sprigs of dill to each jar (1 at the bottom, 1 in the middle, 1 at the top).

In a large enamel or stainless steel pan, combine water, vinegar, and salt and bring to a rolling boil. Immediately pour brine over the cucumbers and seal.　　　　YIELD: *6 quarts*

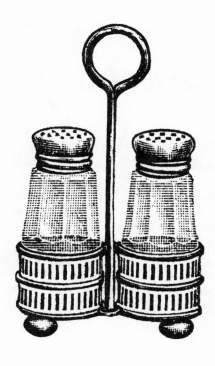

Garlic Pickled Okra

Select only the tender, young okra for this recipe, and the end result will be a crisp pickle that you can eat and eat and eat.

1 pound young, fresh okra
1 cup water
1 cup white vinegar
4 tablespoons whole black
   peppercorns

4 cloves garlic, minced
2 tablespoons salt

Wash okra, leaving stems intact. Pack into 4 sterilized pint jars. Combine water, vinegar, pepper, garlic, and salt in an enamel or stainless steel pan and bring to a boil. Pour into jars and seal immediately. Store in a dark place for at least 2 weeks.

YIELD: *4 pints*

Bread and Butter Pickles

Grandmother always had a good supply of these in the pantry, thank goodness, because they went fast! They are a crunchy pickle and easy to make, so take advantage of a bumper cucumber crop and make enough to last through the winter and some for gift-giving as well.

8 medium cucumbers, thinly
   sliced
4 onions, thinly sliced
¼ cup salt
4 cups cracked ice

2½ cups cider vinegar
2½ cups sugar
2 teaspoons mustard seed
1 teaspoon turmeric

In a large enamel or stainless steel pan, combine cucumber and onion slices, add salt and cracked ice, and cover. Allow to stand for 3–4 hours. Drain and rinse well with ice-cold water. Return to enamel or stainless steel pan and add vinegar, sugar, mustard seed, and turmeric. Cook over medium heat and bring to a boil. Remove from heat immediately. Pack into 5 sterilized pint jars and seal. YIELD: *5 pints*

Corn Relish

One test of a good jelly, pickle, preserve, or relish is whether it looks as good as it tastes. This Corn Relish will pass that test with high marks. And after one bite you will be able to describe the meaning of the word "relishing."

4 cups cooked corn, cut from cob
2 cups shredded cabbage
½ cup chopped bell pepper
½ cup chopped onion
2 cups cider vinegar
1 cup sugar

1 tablespoon dry mustard
1 tablespoon salt
2 teaspoons turmeric
½ cup water
¼ cup chopped pimiento

Combine all ingredients except pimiento into large enamel or stainless steel pan. Cook over high heat and bring to a boil. Reduce heat and simmer uncovered 20–30 minutes, stirring occasionally. Stir in pimiento and pack into pint jars. Seal immediately. YIELD: *3 pints*

Green Tomato Relish

A medley of vegetables, Green Tomato Relish is a tasty condiment, especially when accompanying roasted meats or on a cold roast beef sandwich.

10 green tomatoes, ground coarsely
4 medium onions, chopped

2 tablespoons salt
2 cups white vinegar
2 cups sugar

1 sweet red pepper, chopped
1 green bell pepper, chopped
½ cup chopped celery

1 tablespoon mustard seed
½ teaspoon turmeric

Combine tomatoes, onions, red and green pepper, and celery in a large enamel or stainless steel pan and sprinkle with salt. Let stand overnight. Drain vegetables and set aside. Combine remaining ingredients and boil 15–20 minutes. Add vegetables to vinegar mixture and return to boil for an additional 10–15 minutes. Ladle hot mixture into 6 sterilized pint jars. Seal immediately.

YIELD: *6 pints*

Jalapeño Jelly

An unlikely jelly, granted, but seeing and tasting is believing, and this is really good! Jalapeños really do have a wonderful flavor, and teaming them with the tart lime juice and sugar makes for an interesting taste. The jelly is a lovely green color; when the jar is tied with a red ribbon it makes a beautiful and unique Christmas gift. Serve with breads or as a condiment with meats.

1 green bell pepper, ground
6 fresh jalapeño peppers, ground
1 cup cider vinegar
6 cups sugar

1 6-ounce bottle liquid fruit
   pectin
juice of 1 lime

Combine peppers, vinegar, and sugar in a large enamel or stainless steel pan and boil 3–4 minutes. Remove from heat and add pectin and lime juice. Pour into 6 half-pint sterilized jars and seal.

YIELD: *6 half pints*

Chow Chow

Another green tomato relish, Chow Chow has the added flavor and texture of cabbage.

3 pounds green tomatoes,
  chopped
1 head cabbage, shredded
2 large onions, chopped
2 sweet red peppers, chopped
2 sweet green peppers, chopped

3 cups white vinegar
2 cups sugar
2 tablespoons pickling spice
1 tablespoon mustard seed
1 tablespoon salt

Combine vegetables in a large enamel or stainless steel pan and add remaining ingredients. Toss well and bring to a boil. Lower heat and simmer for 10–15 minutes, stirring occasionally. Pour into 4 hot, sterilized pint jars and seal immediately.

YIELD: *4 pints*

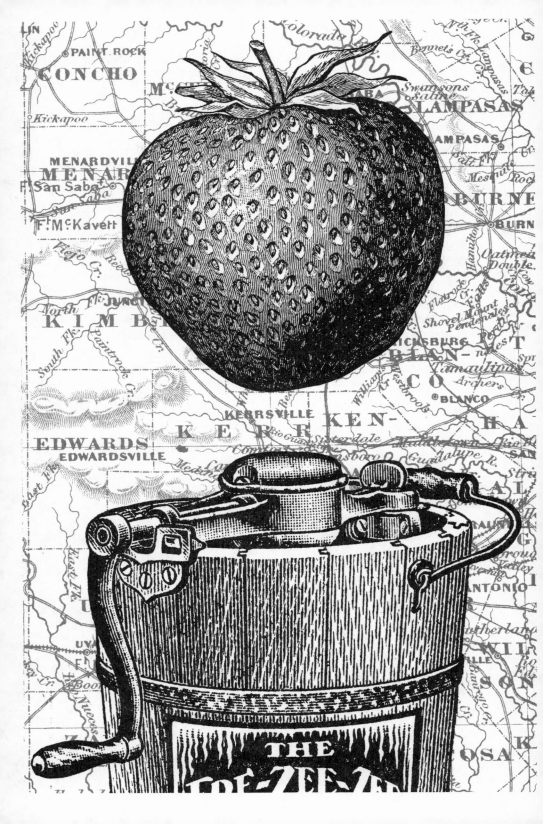

10. Desserts

Brownies

These are delicious plain, sprinkled with powdered sugar, or iced with Fudge Icing. The mix-in-the-pan recipe saves clean-up time and is quick and easy to prepare. Make a double recipe so you can have some on hand in the freezer.

1 cup butter	2 cups sugar
4 ounces unsweetened chocolate	4 eggs, beaten
1 cup flour	1 teaspoon vanilla
1½ teaspoons baking powder	1 cup chopped pecans (optional)

Melt butter and chocolate in a double boiler or heavy saucepan. Sift flour and baking powder into the chocolate mixture; then stir in sugar, eggs, vanilla, and nuts. Pour into a greased 9-by-13-inch baking pan. Bake at 350° for 30 minutes. Let cool, spread with Fudge Icing if desired, and cut into squares.   YIELD: *4 dozen*

Fudge Icing

1 ounce unsweetened chocolate	¼ cup milk
¼ cup shortening	pinch of salt
1 cup sugar	½ teaspoon vanilla

In a saucepan, combine all ingredients except vanilla and slowly bring to a boil. Boil for 1 minute, stirring constantly. Cool and add vanilla.

Using a spoon, beat the icing until it begins to thicken and loses its gloss. (If it gets too thick, add 1 teaspoon milk.)

YIELD: *icing for 4 dozen Brownies*

Butterscotch Brownies

This is another of Grandmother Erben's recipes and one for which she became famous, at least as far as our big clan was concerned. Any time there was a big family reunion or get-together, everyone would bring a dish or two. Whoever was in charge always asked Grandmother to bring her brownies. She would bring a huge, round platter with half Butterscotch Brownies and half iced fudge Brownies (see the preceding recipe).

She happily shared the recipe with anyone who asked her for it, including all the family. But for some reason, when we made the brownies, they never came out quite the same as hers. We would tease her and tell her that she had intentionally left out one ingredient so hers would always be the best, but she insisted that she hadn't.

Now that she is gone, we realize that there is one ingredient missing. It is the love and care that poured from her hands when she mixed the batter.

½ cup butter, softened
2 cups brown sugar
2 eggs
1 cup flour

¾ teaspoon baking powder
1 teaspoon vanilla
½ cup chopped pecans

Cream softened butter, add sugar and eggs, and beat until light and fluffy. Add flour, baking powder, and vanilla and mix well. Stir in nuts.

Spread the batter evenly in a greased and floured 9-by-13-inch baking pan. Bake at 350° for 30–40 minutes. Cool and cut into squares.

YIELD: *4 dozen*

Icebox Cookies

These buttery, crisp cookies are wonderful in taste and convenience. With a roll of dough in the·refrigerator or freezer, you can make a tray of warm cookies any time.

1 cup butter, softened
1 cup brown sugar
1 cup granulated sugar
2 eggs
3½ cups flour

1 teaspoon soda
2 teaspoons cinnamon
½ teaspoon salt
1½ cups pecans, finely chopped

Cream butter and sugars until well blended. Add eggs and beat until the mixture is light and fluffy.

Sift flour, soda, cinnamon, and salt together. Add to the creamed mixture and mix well. Stir in chopped pecans.

Shape the dough into 2 or 3 rolls, 2 inches in diameter. Wrap the rolls in waxed paper or plastic wrap and chill overnight. (The rolls may be left in the refrigerator several days or may be frozen for up to 3 months.)

When ready to bake, slice the cookies very thin, about ¼ inch, and bake on a greased cookie sheet at 400° for 8–10 minutes.

YIELD: *6–7 dozen*

Oatmeal Cookies

Just a hint of nutmeg makes this a very special cookie recipe.

1 cup butter, softened
2 cups sugar
2 eggs
2 cups flour
1 teaspoon baking soda
½ teaspoon cinnamon

¼ teaspoon nutmeg
pinch of salt
2 cups rolled oats
1 cup raisins
1 cup chopped pecans

Combine butter and sugar and cream until light and fluffy. Add eggs and beat well.

Sift flour, soda, cinnamon, nutmeg, and salt together and add to creamed mixture. Stir in oats, raisins, and pecans.

Drop by teaspoonfuls on greased baking sheets and bake at 325° for 10–12 minutes or until golden brown. Cool slightly before removing from pan.   YIELD: *5–6 dozen*

Thumbprint Cookies

Children and cookie baking just seem to go together, maybe because Grandmother, with her divine patience, would always let the little ones help, regardless of the fact that we were always underfoot and made such a mess.

These cookies are perfect for lots of little hands. There is plenty of rolling, dipping, punching, and filling, and the results are delicious.

Make it a special day to remember and invite the children into the kitchen for Thumbprint Cookie making.

1 cup butter, softened	**½ teaspoon salt**
½ cup brown sugar	**1 teaspoon vanilla**
2 eggs, separated	**2 cups pecans, finely chopped**
2 cups flour, sifted	**½ cup jelly or preserves**

Cream softened butter and brown sugar. Add egg yolks and beat until the mixture is light and fluffy. Gradually stir in sifted flour and salt. Add vanilla and mix well. Chill dough about 2 hours or until it is easy to handle.

Beat egg whites until they are frothy. Roll dough into 1-inch balls. Dip each ball into the beaten egg whites and then roll in the chopped pecans, to coat.

Place on a greased baking sheet, 1 inch apart. Using the heel of your thumb or the back of a spoon, make a small depression in the center of each ball. Bake at 375° for 8–10 minutes; remove from oven and press down the centers again with spoon. Return the cookies to oven and continue baking 12–15 minutes. Cool slightly and fill each center with fresh peach, strawberry, or fig preserves or a jelly or preserve of your choice.   YIELD: *4 dozen*

Pecan Sandies

Pecan Sandies are a meringue-type drop cookie that mix up in a flash with an added treat of pecans. There is nothing difficult about making them but, if they are made on a humid day, it is best to store them in an airtight container.

2 egg whites
pinch of salt
½ cup sugar

½ teaspoon vanilla
½ cup chopped pecans

Beat the egg whites and salt until stiff peaks form, gradually adding the sugar. Fold in the vanilla and pecans.

Drop by teaspoonfuls onto a greased baking sheet. Bake at 250° for 20 minutes.   YIELD: *3 dozen*

Grandma's Gingersnaps

Regardless of how many or what kind of desserts are on the table, if Grandma Schmidt has made her Gingersnaps, you can bet it will be the first empty plate. The recipe itself is special, handed down to Grandma from her grandmother before her. There have been a few changes made through the years—Grandma says that her grandmother used lard instead of butter—but essentially it remains the same.

Gingersnaps are a molded cookie with a delicious ginger flavor. When baked, the cookies flatten to perfect circles with tiny hairline cracks on the top; these cracks give them the traditional Gingersnap appearance. When you bite into one, it is crisp around the edges with just a hint of softness in the middle.

In this hectic world in which we live, few of us have the time or patience required to make cookies like Grandma's. They may taste almost the same, but we may burn one batch, or they may not all be perfectly round and the same size as hers are.

Grandma takes special pride in making these cookies, and well she should, for they are high in demand! It is not only because the "'snaps" (as her grandchildren and great-grandchildren call them) are so good. It is also because she adds her special touch of love and care to each batch that she makes.

¾ cup butter, melted
1 cup sugar
¼ cup unsulphured molasses
1 egg
2 cups flour

1 teaspoon baking soda
½ teaspoon ground cloves
¾ teaspoon ground ginger
¾ teaspoon cinnamon
½ teaspoon salt

Combine cooled melted butter with sugar, molasses, and egg and mix well. Sift the remaining ingredients together and stir into the sugar mixture.

Cover the dough and refrigerate for several hours. When chilled, roll into 1-inch balls and roll each ball in granulated sugar. Place the balls on a greased cookie sheet 2 inches apart. Flatten each ball with the bottom of a glass which has been dipped in granulated sugar. Bake at 375° for 8–10 minutes. Remove from pans immediately and cool on wire racks.   YIELD: *5 dozen*

Bizcochitos

The Mexicans have a delightful Christmas custom, which has been carried over into Texas, called "Las Posadas." A group of carolers portray the Holy Family in search of a room for the night. As they approach each house they sing a song to the occupant explaining their predicament and asking for lodging. The occupants in each house reply in song that there is no room. The pilgrimage and songs continue until the carolers reach the last house, where indeed there is room. Here all the participants gather in celebration of the event. The festivities will most likely include Mexican Hot Chocolate (Chapter 2) and Bizcochitos—a traditional Mexican lard cookie which is light, flaky, and delicious.

1 cup lard or shortening
¾ cup sugar
1 egg

2 teaspoons cinnamon
¼ cup water (a sweet wine or
    fruit juice may be substituted)

3 cups flour   ¼ cup sugar
1½ teaspoons baking powder   ½ teaspoon cinnamon
½ teaspoon salt

Cream lard and sugar together until smooth. Add egg and beat
until light and fluffy.

Sift together flour, baking powder, salt, and 2 teaspoons cinnamon. Slowly add to the lard mixture, alternately with water.
Mix until well blended.

Cover and refrigerate until well chilled, at least 4 hours or
overnight.

Roll out a small portion of the chilled dough on a floured board.
Keep remaining dough refrigerated. Roll very thin, about ⅛ inch
thick, and cut with cookie cutters into desired shapes. Dough may
also be cut with a knife into random shapes.

Place on an ungreased cookie sheet and bake at 375° for 10–15
minutes. Remove from oven and dip each cookie in a mixture of ¼
cup sugar and ½ teaspoon cinnamon.

YIELD: *6 dozen 2-inch cookies*

Buñuelo Rosettes

Buñuelos are a crisp fried pastry covered with cinnamon and
sugar. Traditionally they are made from a sweet dough which is
formed into small balls, rolled wafer-thin, and deep fried. A variation of these are Buñuelo Rosettes. They are similar to timbales,
made with a sweet, thin batter and a rosette iron. Be sure to make
a big batch, for they are light and airy and melt in your mouth like
cotton candy. Store them in an air-tight container and they will
keep for several weeks.

2 eggs, slightly beaten   1 teaspoon lemon or almond
2 teaspoons sugar   extract
¼ teaspoon salt   oil for frying
1 cup milk   ½ cup sugar
1 cup flour   1 teaspoon cinnamon

In a small mixing bowl, combine beaten eggs, 2 teaspoons sugar, salt, and milk. Add flour and mix with a wire whisk or fork until smooth. Stir in extract. The batter will be about the consistency of heavy cream. In a separate bowl, mix ½ cup sugar and cinnamon and set aside.

Heat 3 inches of oil in a heavy saucepan to 375°. Dip a rosette iron in the oil to heat it. When heated, dip the iron into the batter, being careful not to let the batter run over the top of the iron. Immerse the batter-coated iron into the oil. After 10–15 seconds, the buñuelo will slip off the iron. Fry for 10–15 seconds more, turning once or twice, until it is golden brown. Remove and drain on paper towels and sprinkle with cinnamon-sugar mixture. Repeat process until all batter is used.   YIELD: *6 dozen*

Sopaipillas

Sopaipillas could be described as Mexican doughnuts. When deep fried, they puff up to make a light, airy treat. They are either sprinkled with cinnamon and sugar or served warm with honey. To eat with honey, break off a corner of the sopaipilla and drizzle the honey inside. The result is messy and wonderful.

2–2½ cups flour	**2 tablespoons lard or shortening**
½ teaspoon salt	**¾ cup warm water**
¼ cup sugar	**oil for frying**
2½ teaspoons baking powder	

Sift flour, salt, sugar, and baking powder together. Cut in lard or shortening until the mixture looks like coarse cornmeal. Add water gradually, mixing until you have a stiff dough. Add more flour if needed.

Turn the dough out onto a floured board. Knead the dough 3–4 minutes or until it is smooth and no longer sticky. Cover and allow to rest for 20–30 minutes.

Roll the dough out on a floured board to ¼-inch thickness. Cut into 1-inch squares.

Heat 2 inches of oil in a heavy saucepan to 385°. Drop 2 or 3 squares of dough into oil. Fry 30–60 seconds, turning several times, or until they are golden brown. Drain on paper towels.

YIELD: *2 dozen*

Peach Tassies

Peach Tassies are small tarts made with a rich cream cheese dough and a "peachy" filling. The dough is formed in muffin tins, baked, and then filled. They are a showy as well as delicious treat.

3 ounces cream cheese, softened
½ cup butter, softened
3 tablespoons sugar

1 teaspoon lemon juice
1½ cups flour
Peach Filling (see below)

Combine cream cheese, butter, sugar, and lemon juice and beat until light and fluffy. Gradually add flour, mixing until a soft dough forms. Refrigerate for 20–30 minutes. (For food processor, process as above, until dough forms a ball.)

Roll dough into 24 balls ¾–1 inch in diameter. Press into cups or small muffin or tassie tins to ¼-inch thickness. Bake at 375° for 10 minutes. Remove from oven and press down center of each tassie. Return to oven and continue baking for 8–10 minutes or until golden brown.

Cool, remove from tins, and fill with Peach Filling.

YIELD: *2 dozen*

PEACH FILLING

4 tablespoons cornstarch
4 tablespoons sugar
pinch of salt

2 cups fresh peach puree
2–4 tablespoons sugar
1 tablespoon butter

In a medium saucepan, combine cornstarch, 4 tablespoons sugar, and salt. Sweeten peach puree with 2–4 tablespoons sugar and gradually add to cornstarch mixture, blending until smooth.

Bring peach mixture to a boil over medium heat, stirring constantly, and cook about 5 minutes, until mixture is thickened. Remove from heat and stir in butter. Cool slightly and spoon into tassie shells.

Mango Meringues

The light, delicate, cloudlike meringue cups are surpassed only by the mango filling: truly a heavenly dessert.

6 egg whites, at room
   temperature
¼ teaspoon cream of tartar
1½ cups sugar
1 teaspoon vanilla

3–4 cups sliced fresh mangoes
2 tablespoons lime juice
1¾ cups sweetened condensed
   milk
½ cup whipped cream

Beat egg whites until foamy and add cream of tartar. Gradually add sugar while beating and continue until stiff peaks form.

Cover two cookie sheets with aluminum foil. Drop meringue by spoonfuls to make 12 mounds about 2½ inches in diameter, spaced 2 inches apart (6 on each sheet). With the back of a spoon, make a well in the middle of each mound. Bake at 250° for 1 hour or until firm. Turn off the oven and leave meringues for several hours.

In a food processor or blender, puree the mangoes. Add lime juice and condensed milk and blend. Chill for several hours.

When ready to serve, fold whipped cream into mango mixture and spoon into meringue shells. Garnish with a thin twist of lime, if desired.   YIELD: *12 servings*

Chocolate Sheet Cake

Chocolate lovers beware—here is an irresistible temptation. The cake is iced while it is still warm so that it absorbs some of the nutty, chocolate flavor. It is a good cake to take to a picnic or bazaar because it is served from the baking pan. Just ice it, cover it, and you're on your way.

2 cups flour
2 cups sugar
½ cup butter (or margarine)
½ cup shortening
4 tablespoons cocoa
1 cup water
½ cup buttermilk

2 eggs, slightly beaten
1 teaspoon salt
1 teaspoon baking soda
1 teaspoon cinnamon
1 teaspoon vanilla
icing (see p. 166)

Sift flour and sugar together into a large mixing bowl and set aside. Combine butter, shortening, cocoa, and water in a saucepan and slowly bring to a boil. Pour the cocoa mixture over the flour and sugar and mix well. Stir in buttermilk, eggs, salt, soda, cinnamon, and vanilla.

Pour into a greased and floured 9-by-13-inch baking pan and bake at 350° for 35 minutes.

Begin making the icing 5 minutes before the cake is done. Allow the cake to cool about 5 minutes and ice while it is still warm.
YIELD: *1 9-by-13-inch cake*

ICING

½ cup butter (or margarine)
4 tablespoons cocoa
6 tablespoons milk

3½ cups powdered sugar, sifted
1 teaspoon vanilla
1 cup chopped pecans

In a medium saucepan, combine butter, cocoa, and milk and slowly bring to a boil. Remove from heat and add the powdered sugar, mixing well. Stir in vanilla and nuts.

YIELD: *icing for 1 9-by-13-inch cake*

Skillet Upside-down Cake

When this cake is taken from the oven and the skillet is turned over, the cake is iced, decorated, and ready to eat.

⅓ cup vegetable oil
1 egg
⅔ cup milk
1⅓ cups sifted flour
1 cup sugar
2 teaspoons baking powder
½ teaspoon salt

1 teaspoon vanilla
6–8 tablespoons butter
¾ cup brown sugar
6 slices canned pineapple
maraschino cherries (optional)
pecan halves (optional)

Using an electric mixer, blend oil, egg, and milk. Sift flour, sugar, baking powder, and salt together and add to the milk mixture. Beat on medium speed for 2 minutes. Stir in vanilla and beat 1 more minute.

In a 10-inch heavy iron skillet, melt 6–8 tablespoons butter. When butter has melted, sprinkle ¾ cup brown sugar evenly over the bottom of the pan. Arrange pineapple slices on top of sugar mixture. Decorate with cherries and/or pecan halves, if desired.

Carefully pour cake batter into skillet over fruit mixture. Bake at 350° for 45–50 minutes or until a toothpick inserted in the center comes out clean. Immediately turn the cake upside down on serving plate. Leave the skillet over the cake for several minutes, then remove.

YIELD: *1 10-inch cake*

1-2-3-4 Cake

Recipe books were scarce in pioneer Texas, and cooks had to memorize the recipes they wanted. One recipe that anyone could remember began with 1 cup butter, 2 cups sugar, 3 cups flour, and 4 eggs.

1 cup butter	3 teaspoons baking powder
2 cups sugar	½ teaspoon salt
3 cups flour	1 cup milk
4 eggs	1 teaspoon lemon extract

Combine butter and sugar and cream until light and fluffy. Add eggs one at a time and beat until smooth.

Sift flour, baking powder, and salt together. Add to creamed mixture alternately with milk. Stir in lemon extract.

Pour into a greased and floured 9-inch tube pan and bake at 350° for 1¼ hours. Remove from oven and cool in pan for 10–15 minutes. Turn out and cool thoroughly on a wire rack.

YIELD: *1 9-inch tube cake*

Pecan Cake

This cake meets all the requirements for a perfect holiday cake: it is pretty to look at, it keeps well, and the bourbon flavor gives it a festive taste. Don't forget about the rest of the year, though. Pack it in a tin for a hostess gift or as a treat to make a sick friend feel better.

½ cup butter, softened	¼ teaspoon salt
¾ cup sugar	1 teaspoon nutmeg
2 eggs, beaten	½ cup bourbon
1½ cups flour	2 cups chopped pecans
1 teaspoon baking powder	1 cup raisins

Combine softened butter and sugar and cream until light and fluffy. Stir in beaten eggs.

Sift flour, baking powder, salt, and nutmeg together and stir into creamed mixture alternately with bourbon. Fold in pecans and raisins.

Spread batter into a greased and floured 10-inch tube pan and bake at 325° for 1½ hours. Cool on a wire rack before removing from pan.   YIELD: *1 10-inch tube cake*

Strawberry Shortcake

About 30 miles south of San Antonio is the small town of Poteet, the strawberry capital of Texas. The red, sandy soil of this area is conducive to growing large, luscious berries, and Texans all over the state wait anxiously for them to arrive in their local markets. When they begin to come in, one of the first things made is Strawberry Shortcake.

2 cups sliced fresh strawberries	**½ teaspoon salt**
¼–½ cup sugar	**¾ cup milk**
2 cups flour	**½ cup butter, melted**
4 teaspoons baking powder	**whipped cream (optional)**
¼ cup sugar	**8 whole strawberries (optional)**

In a small bowl, combine sliced strawberries and ¼–½ cup sugar (amount depending on the sweetness of the strawberries) and refrigerate.

Sift flour, baking powder, ¼ cup sugar, and salt together. Add milk and melted butter and mix until moistened. Spread into a greased 9-inch square baking pan. Bake at 450° for 15 minutes.

To serve, cut shortcake into 8 squares. Split each square in half with a fork. Spoon strawberries over bottom half of shortcake and cover with top half. If desired, garnish with a dollop of whipped cream and top with a whole fresh berry or a spoonful of strawberry juice.   YIELD: *8 servings*

Spice Cake

The sweet spice smells that fill the kitchen while this cake is baking conjure up thoughts of autumn leaves and cool, brisk breezes.

Bake it in celebration of fall's arrival or any time you have a yen for a mild, sweet, spicy taste. For the "icing on the cake," the caramel flavor is delectable.

¾ **cup shortening**
¾ **cup sugar**
¾ **cup brown sugar**
3 **eggs**
1¾ **cup flour**
½ **teaspoon baking powder**
½ **teaspoon baking soda**
½ **teaspoon salt**

1 **teaspoon ground cloves**
½ **teaspoon nutmeg**
1 **teaspoon cinnamon**
¾ **cup buttermilk**
1 **teaspoon vanilla**
1 **cup finely chopped pecans**
Caramel Icing (see below)

Combine shortening and sugars and cream until light and fluffy. Add eggs, one at a time, and beat well.

Sift flour, baking powder, soda, salt, cloves, nutmeg, and cinnamon together. Gradually add to egg mixture alternately with buttermilk, mixing until well blended. Stir in vanilla and nuts.

Pour into a greased and floured 9-by-13-inch baking pan and bake at 375° for 35–40 minutes. Remove from oven and cool. Ice with Caramel Icing.   YIELD: *1 9-by-13-inch cake*

Caramel Icing

½ **cup butter**
½ **cup brown sugar**

2 **tablespoons evaporated milk**
¾–1 **cup powdered sugar**

In a small saucepan, melt butter, add brown sugar, and cook over low heat 2–3 minutes. Gradually add milk and bring mixture to a boil. Remove from heat and cool slightly.

Add powdered sugar, a little at a time, beating until smooth. If icing is too thick, add 1 teaspoon milk.

YIELD: *Icing for 1 9-by-13-inch cake*

Sweet Potato Cake

Next time you are baking sweet potatoes, put a couple of extra ones in the oven to use later for an old time favorite—Sweet Potato Cake with Butter-Nut Cream Icing.

½ cup shortening
¾ cup sugar
¾ cup brown sugar
2 eggs
2 cups flour
3 teaspoons baking powder
½ teaspoon salt
¼ teaspoon baking soda

1½ teaspoons cinnamon
¾ cup buttermilk
1 cup mashed cooked sweet potato (or yams)
½ cup chopped nuts
Butter-Nut Cream Icing (see below)

Combine shortening and sugars and cream until light. Add eggs and mix well.

Sift flour, baking powder, salt, soda, and cinnamon together and gradually add to creamed mixture alternately with buttermilk. Add mashed sweet potato and nuts and mix well. Bake at 350° in a greased and floured 9-by-13-inch pan for 40–45 minutes or in two 9-inch round pans for 30-35 minutes. Ice with Butter-Nut Cream Icing.
YIELD: *1 9-by-13-inch cake or 2 9-inch layers*

Butter-Nut Cream Icing

⅓ cup butter, softened
3 cups powdered sugar
pinch of salt

¼ cup evaporated milk
1½ teaspoons vanilla
½ cup finely chopped pecans

Cream butter, 1 cup powdered sugar, and salt until fluffy. Add remaining sugar alternately with milk and mix until smooth. Stir in vanilla and pecans.
YIELD: *Icing for 1 9-by-13-inch cake or 2 9-inch layer cakes*

Sour Cream Apple Pie

Any lover of apple pie will enjoy this hearty, rich variation of America's favorite.

9 tart apples
1¼ cups sugar
½ cup flour
½ teaspoon cinnamon
1 10-inch unbaked pie crust

½ cup sour cream
2 tablespoons butter
2 tablespoons lemon juice
2 tablespoons sugar
cinnamon to taste

Peel and slice apples and place in a large bowl. Combine 1¼ cups sugar, ½ cup flour, and ½ teaspoon cinnamon and add to sliced apples. Toss until all apples are well coated.

Line the bottom of the pie crust with about a third of the apples. Spoon half of the sour cream over the apples. Add another layer of apples and remaining sour cream. Top with remaining apples. Dot with butter and drizzle lemon juice over all. Sprinkle 2 tablespoons sugar and cinnamon as desired over the top.

Bake at 350° for 15 minutes. Lower heat to 325° and continue baking for about 1 hour, or until apples are tender and the top is lightly browned.   YIELD: *1 10-inch pie*

Buttermilk Pie

A smooth, creamy, delicious pie, and a recipe worth trying—despite any preconceived notions you may have about buttermilk. Originally this pie was a makeshift dessert for times when the pantry or cellar was bare and there were no fruits in season. It has now become much more—a classic Texas dessert.

4 tablespoons flour
1¾ cups sugar
½ teaspoon salt
½ cup butter, melted
3 eggs, beaten
1 cup buttermilk

½ teaspoon vanilla
½ teaspoon lemon extract
9-inch unbaked pie shell
cinnamon and nutmeg to taste
  (optional)

Combine flour, sugar, and salt in a mixing bowl. Add melted butter and beaten eggs and stir with a whisk or fork until well blended. Stir in buttermilk, vanilla, and lemon extract and mix well. Pour into unbaked pie shell and dust with cinnamon or nutmeg, if desired.

Bake in center of 350° oven for 55–60 minutes or until filling is set and lightly browned.   YIELD: *1 9-inch pie*

Lemon Meringue Pie

A standard all-time favorite.

1½ cups sugar
½ cup cornstarch
dash of salt
1¾ cups water
4 egg yolks, beaten
½ cup lemon juice
1 teaspoon grated lemon rind

2 tablespoons butter
1 9-inch baked pie shell
4 egg whites, at room
   temperature
¼ teaspoon cream of tartar
dash of salt
½ cup sugar

In a large saucepan, combine 1½ cups sugar, cornstarch, and salt and mix well. Gradually add water, stirring constantly until smooth. Cook over medium high heat and continue stirring for about 5 minutes until mixture has thickened enough to mound and is beginning to bubble but not quite boil. Reduce heat to low and cook an additional 2–3 minutes, stirring constantly.

Add a small amount of the hot sugar mixture to the beaten egg yolks. Add the yolk mixture to the pan and cook over a very low heat for 2–3 minutes, stirring constantly. Do not allow mixture to boil. Cool slightly.

Slowly stir in lemon juice, grated rind, and butter; stir until butter melts. Spoon filling into the baked pie shell and set aside while preparing meringue.

In a small metal bowl, beat egg whites until foamy. Add cream of tartar and a dash of salt and continue beating, adding ½ cup sugar gradually, until stiff peaks form.

Spread meringue over filling, being sure meringue touches and adheres to edges of crust. Bake at 375° for 10–12 minutes or until meringue is lightly browned. Cool to room temperature before serving.   YIELD: *1 9-inch pie*

Sweet Potato Pie

Texas has more fairs and festivals than any other state—well over 500 annually. From the Texas Rose Festival in Tyler to Buccaneer Days in Corpus Christi, from the Watermelon Thump in Luling to the Southwestern Sun Carnival in El Paso—Texans can always find a reason to celebrate.

One such celebration is the Yamboree held each October in Gilmer—the sweet potato capital of Texas and the place of origin of this Sweet Potato Pie. It is definitely a "blue ribbon" winner.

½ cup finely chopped pecans
2 tablespoons butter, softened
¼ cup brown sugar
9-inch unbaked pie shell
1 cup mashed sweet potato
¾ cup dark corn syrup

4 tablespoons butter
½ cup brown sugar
2 teaspoons cornstarch
½ teaspoon salt
3 eggs, beaten
15–20 pecan halves

Combine ½ cup nuts, 2 tablespoons butter, and ¼ cup brown sugar and spread on the bottom of the unbaked pie shell. Bake at 450° for 10 minutes; remove from oven and cool.

In a medium saucepan, combine mashed sweet potato, corn syrup, 4 tablespoons butter, ½ cup brown sugar, cornstarch, and salt. Bring to a boil and cook for 3 minutes, stirring constantly. Slowly add beaten eggs and mix well.

Pour into pie shell and decorate the top with the pecan halves. Bake at 400° for 10 minutes. Reduce heat to 350° and continue baking for 30–35 minutes or until set.   YIELD: *1 9-inch pie*

Pecan Pie

It seems that wherever our grandparents lived they always had big, beautiful pecan trees growing in their yard. Grandpa had a special green thumb for them, as he did with anything he grew, and he always had a bountiful harvest. He also had a special trick when it came to cracking and shelling the nuts. The pecans would always come out of the shell in two perfect halves. The grandchildren would sit outside with him and "help" him shell the nuts, but when we got a perfect half it was by sheer luck.

It was the pecan halves which made the best pecan pies. They really didn't taste any different, but they looked so nice because Grandmother would arrange the halves in a design on the top.

3 eggs, lightly beaten
½ cup sugar
1 cup light corn syrup
1 cup pecans

pinch of salt
1 teaspoon vanilla
9-inch unbaked pie shell

Combine eggs, sugar, and syrup and blend well. Stir in pecans, salt, and vanilla.

Pour the mixture into the unbaked pie shell and bake at 425° for 10 minutes. Lower the heat to 350° and continue baking for 20 minutes or until the filling is firm and the crust is lightly browned.

YIELD: *1 9-inch pie*

Wild Mustang Green Grape Pie

Wild Mustang Green Grape Pie is a true treat from Texas past, and it is still enjoyed today by those of us who have access to a place where the delicate grapes can be picked. Grandma said that her mother made a cobbler with the grapes because a pie would not go around their large family of five boys and three girls. She said that the trick for a perfect pie was to pick the grapes at just the right time, while they were still a luscious green color and just before the seed formed.

3 cups green mustang grapes
1½ cups sugar
3 tablespoons flour
3 tablespoons butter

unbaked pastry for a 9-inch two-
   crust pie
¼ cup melted butter (optional)
sprinkling of sugar (optional)

Wash the grapes and put in a saucepan with just enough water to cover; bring to a slow boil.

Combine the sugar and flour and add to the grapes when they begin to boil. Add butter and cook over medium heat, stirring gently, about 5 minutes, until the mixture begins to thicken.

Pour into an unbaked 9-inch pie crust and top with a lattice crust. Brush the top crust with a little melted butter and a sprinkling of sugar, if desired.

Bake at 400° for 10 minutes. Reduce heat to 325° and continue baking for 20–30 minutes.   YIELD: *1 9-inch pie*

Bread Pudding

"Waste not, want not," we were often told. A good way not to waste any stale bread or cake is to make a Bread Pudding. You will be rewarded for being frugal with a delicious dessert. It may not sound like a dessert fit for a king, but when topped with Lemon Sauce or Custard Sauce (see Chapter 7 for recipes), it can rival anything from a royal baker.

6 cups dry bread or cake, broken
   into small pieces and firmly
   packed
½ cup raisins

3 cups milk, scalded
¼–½ cup sugar
4 eggs, beaten
1 teaspoon vanilla

In a buttered 2-quart casserole, combine bread or cake and raisins and toss to distribute evenly. To the scalded milk, add ¼–½ cup sugar, depending on sweetness of bread or cake used. Add beaten egg and vanilla to milk, mix well, and pour over bread or cake pieces.

Bake at 350° for 40–45 minutes, or until pudding begins to brown and is firm.   YIELD: *8–10 servings*

Peach Cobbler

The Edwards Plateau is a rocky, hilly region affectionately known to Texans as the Hill Country, and it is there that the best peaches are grown. The peach harvest is celebrated with county fairs and festivals and roadside stands where the fruit can be bought by the bushel basket.

A favorite way to use these peaches is in a cobbler—a dessert that is easier to make than a pie and works especially well for a crowd. Serve warm with a scoop of ice cream.

FILLING

5 tablespoons cornstarch
2–2½ cups sugar
8 cups sliced fresh peaches

½ teaspoon almond extract
¼ cup butter, melted

PASTRY

½ cup shortening
2 cups flour
2 tablespoons sugar
pinch of salt

4–5 tablespoons ice water
3 tablespoons butter, melted
2 tablespoons sugar

To prepare filling, blend cornstarch and sugar (amount depending on the tartness of the peaches) together and toss with peaches, almond extract, and melted butter and set aside.

For pastry, cut shortening into flour until it is the consistency of cornmeal. Add 2 tablespoons sugar and salt. Gradually add ice water until the dough holds its shape. Roll out on a floured board and cut into 5 1-by-13-inch strips and 7 1-by-9-inch strips.

Pour filling in a buttered 9-by-13-inch baking pan. Crisscross dough strips over filling. Brush dough with melted butter and sprinkle with sugar. Bake at 400° for 30 minutes or until crust is browned.   YIELD: *10–12 servings*

German Rice Pudding

Rice pudding is now generally thought of as a way to use any leftover rice. But it hasn't always been so, and once you have tried making it from scratch, it probably won't be again.

2 cups water	**½ cup sugar**
½ teaspoon salt	**½ cup raisins (optional)**
½ cup uncooked long-grain rice	**1 teaspoon vanilla**
3 cups milk	**cinnamon to taste (optional)**
1 tablespoon butter	

In a large saucepan, bring water and salt to a rolling boil. Add rice and return to boil. Reduce heat and continue cooking until water is absorbed and rice is tender.

In another saucepan, combine milk and butter. Cook over low heat until butter has melted and milk is scalded.

Pour milk into cooked rice. Simmer for 15–20 minutes, stirring occasionally. Sprinkle mixture with sugar and add raisins if desired. Cook over medium heat for an additional 15–20 minutes or until mixture is creamy. Stir in vanilla.

Serve warm, sprinkled with cinnamon if desired.

YIELD: *6 servings*

Flan

This classic Mexican custard with its delicate caramel sauce is a wonderful ending to a Tex-Mex meal or any time a smooth, light dessert is called for.

1 cup sugar	**¾ cup sugar**
5 eggs, beaten	**1 cup heavy cream**
1¾ cups evaporated milk	**2 teaspoons vanilla**

In a 10-inch round metal pan (at least 1½ inches deep), sprinkle 1 cup sugar. Place pan over low heat and stir sugar constantly until it melts and turns golden brown. Immediately tip and turn pan to coat bottom and sides completely. Set aside.

In a mixing bowl, combine beaten eggs, evaporated milk, ¾ cup sugar, cream, and vanilla. Pour into caramelized pan and place in a larger pan of warm water.

Bake at 350° for 75–85 minutes or until flan is firm and a knife inserted in center comes out clean.

Remove from oven and allow to cool for 10–15 minutes. (Do not allow to cool any longer, or caramel sauce will harden and remain in pan.)

Invert onto a large serving dish, with rim.

Chill several hours before serving. YIELD: *8–10 servings*

Strawberry Ice Cream

What is better than a gathering of friends and homemade ice cream? On the Fourth of July, after a cattle auction, or at a church social, everyone can gather around and take turns cranking the freezer. It is a shame to use an electric freezer, since half of the fun is cranking it to just the right degree and swapping tales while waiting for it to set. Then, too, there is the reward of licking the paddles when all the work is done.

4 pints fresh strawberries	**1 teaspoon vanilla**
5 eggs	**dash of salt**
2 cups sugar	**crushed ice**
2 cups heavy cream	**ice cream salt**
2 cups milk	

Wash and hull strawberries. Puree in a blender or food processor and set aside.

Beat eggs until foamy and add sugar, cream, milk, vanilla, and salt. Mix until well blended. Stir in pureed fruit.

Pour into a 1-gallon ice cream freezer to within 3–4 inches from top. Pack freezer with 6 parts ice to 1 part ice cream salt and freeze.   YIELD: *1 gallon*

Mango Ice Cream

Mangoes are a tropical fruit very popular in Mexico and Texas. The fresh fruit vendors in Mexico peel them and insert a stick, and they are eaten like popsicles. Mangoes are also wonderful in pies and ice cream.

4 large eggs
1 cup sugar
1¾ cups sweetened condensed
  milk
1½ quarts milk
1 tablespoon vanilla

2 cups canned mangoes, drained
  and mashed
1 tablespoon lime juice
ice cream salt
ice

Using an electric mixer, beat eggs on high speed for 4 minutes. Add sugar and condensed milk and beat an additional 2 minutes. Stir in milk and vanilla. Add mangoes and lime juice. Pour into a 1-gallon ice cream freezer to within 3–4 inches from top. Pack freezer with 1 part ice cream salt to 6 parts ice and freeze.

YIELD: *1 gallon*

VARIATIONS

Fresh Mango Ice Cream. Substitute 2 cups fresh mangoes, thinly sliced, for canned mangoes. Increase sugar to 1½ cups. Proceed as directed.

Peach Ice Cream. Substitute 2 cups fresh peaches, thinly sliced, for mangoes. Omit lime juice and increase sugar to 1½ cups. Proceed as directed.

Pralines

Almost every Tex-Mex meal seems to end with a praline. They are a good dessert choice when you're feeding a crowd: arrange them on a tray or in a basket and let your guests help themselves. You will find that the buttery taste is just right, and they will melt in your mouth.

2 cups sugar
1 teaspoon baking soda
pinch of salt
1 cup buttermilk

2 tablespoons butter
1½–2 cups pecans
1 teaspoon vanilla

In a large saucepan, combine sugar, soda, salt, and buttermilk. Cook over high heat, stirring constantly, to bring the mixture to a boil. Continue boiling and stirring until it begins to thicken and to take on a creamy tinge. It should be about 210° on a candy thermometer at this time.

Add butter and pecans and continue cooking over medium high heat until it reaches 234° on candy thermometer (soft ball stage). Remove from heat, stir in vanilla, and allow to cool slightly—about 2 minutes.

Beat the mixture until it begins to lose its gloss and is thick and creamy. Quickly drop into 2-inch mounds on waxed paper and allow to cool. If the mixture becomes too hard, immerse pan in hot water for several minutes and proceed.   YIELD: *2 dozen*

Divinity

Divinity is just what the name suggests—divine. We always make it at Christmastime—the candy-making season. Don't let the fact that it is a candy scare you off. It is no more difficult than stirring up a batch of cookies. So, when December rolls around, give it a try. It is best to make it on a cool, dry day. Place it in air-tight containers and it will keep for 7–10 days—or package it and give it for gifts.

2½ cups sugar
¾ cup white corn syrup
¼ cup water
2 egg whites

¼ cup sugar
1 teaspoon vanilla
1 cup chopped pecans

Combine 2½ cups sugar, corn syrup, and water in a saucepan and bring to a boil, stirring constantly. Continue boiling, without stirring, until the mixture spins small threads from the spoon (254°). Remove from heat.

Beat egg whites until stiff, gradually adding ¼ cup sugar. Pour the boiled mixture slowly into the egg whites, beating constantly. Stir in vanilla and chopped pecans.

Immediately drop by teaspoonfuls onto waxed paper and allow to cool.   YIELD: *3–4 dozen*

Candied Pecans

In this recipe, pecans, the glorious gift of the state tree of Texas, are combined with a cinnamon-flavored coating to make a truly memorable confection.

1 cup sugar
¾ teaspoon salt
1½ teaspoons cinnamon

½ cup water
1 teaspoon vanilla
½ pound pecan halves

In a 10-inch skillet, combine sugar, salt, and cinnamon; add water, mixing until well blended. Cook over medium high heat, stirring constantly, about 4 minutes, until thin threads spin from the spoon (254°). Remove from heat, add vanilla, and gently stir in pecans; stir 3–5 minutes, until pecans are well coated and the syrup begins to lose its gloss.

Turn out on waxed paper, carefully separating each nut, and allow to cool. Store in air-tight containers.   YIELD: *3 cups*

Index